WHY BELIEVE IN JESUS?

A LIFE WORTH INVESTIGATING

GUILLERMO MALDONADO

WHITAKER
HOUSE

Our Mission

Called to bring the supernatural power of God to this generation

Project Director: Addilena Torres
General Editor: Jacqueline Delgado
Cover Design: Danielle Cruz-Nieri
Interior Design: José M. Anhuaman

Why Believe in Jesus?

Guillermo Maldonado
13651 S.W. 143rd Ct., #101
Miami, FL 33186
http://kingjesusministry.org/
www.ERJPub.org

ISBN: 978-1-62911-310-4
eBook ISBN: 978-1-62911-311-1
Printed in the United States of America
© 2015 by Guillermo Maldonado

Whitaker House
1030 Hunt Valley Circle
New Kensington, PA 15068
www.whitakerhouse.com

4 5 6 7 8 9 10   ⨆⨆   21 20 19 18 17 16 15

Dedication

I dedicate this book to all the people around the world who long for a personal relationship with the living Jesus, who gave His life for us, and was resurrected by God, the Father. I dedicate it to the chosen people of God, who urgently need an accurate answer to the question: Why believe in Jesus? I also dedicate it to the Bride—the Church— who is preparing for the wedding feast of the Lamb.

I dedicate this book to Jesus, the only Way, Truth, and Life. Praise be to the only wise God, our Savior, who sits on the throne, and to the Lamb. Only He is worthy of praise, worship, honor, glory, power, and majesty.

This book is to exalt You, Jesus, Son of God most high!

Contents

Introduction

His life was designated a milestone in human history— dividing it into two distinct periods: before Christ (B.C. or B.C.E.) and after Christ (A.D. or C.E.). In many parts of the world, His birth is celebrated during the season of Christmas, and His death and resurrection are commemorated on Good Friday and Easter Sunday. More books have been written about Him than any other person who has ever lived. His words and deeds are reverenced by hundreds of millions. Over the centuries, many have given up their lives rather than deny their allegiance to Him. And people from ancient times to the present have considered His life a mystery worthy of being investigated.

Yet, even today, the person of Jesus Christ evokes mixed responses from people. Many admire and believe in Him as the Son of God. Some view Him as a loving and generous historical personage. Certain people consider Him an enlightened prophet, a wise man, or a spiritual guide. Others barely think about Him, recognizing Him only as a character they have seen in a movie, or using His name as a curse word. Some people are skeptical about His existence and His claims. Still others seem to hate Him, even to the point of persecuting those who follow His teachings.

What is it about Jesus' life, claims, and teachings that attract many people's attention and either win their devotion or awaken great opposition to Him? It is not difficult to accept the fact that Jesus was a historical figure who walked on this earth two millennia ago. Yet who was He? Where did He come from? What did He teach?

If He truly was a Savior, in what way does that reality affect us today, so many centuries later? What does He currently mean to us, and how should we respond to Him? In the following pages, we will explore these questions as we seek answers to the central question, *Why Believe in Jesus?*

1

An Invitation

Jesus Christ was thirty years old when He began to travel to various towns in His region and teach. His message was characterized by a series of invitations to people. He would say things like, "Follow Me,"[1] "If anyone thirsts, let him come to Me and drink. He who believes in Me, as the Scripture has said, out of his heart will flow rivers of living water,"[2] and "Come to me, all you who are weary and burdened, and I will give you rest. Take my yoke upon you and learn from me, for I am gentle and humble in heart, and you will find rest for your souls."[3]

The people to whom He spoke were living in turbulent social and political times. Many of them were looking for purpose, peace, and power in their lives. They wanted genuine solutions to their everyday difficulties as they dealt with their personal relationships, health, finances, and so on.

Seeking What Is Real and Lasting

Similarly, most people in our contemporary world are seeking something real for their lives, perhaps more than at any other time in history. Our world is filled with uncertainty. Throughout our planet, we face financial crises, political upheaval, natural disasters, wars, terrorism, crime, widespread hunger and disease,

---

[1] See, for example, Mark 1:17; 2:14.
[2] John 7:37.
[3] Matthew 11:28–29 (NIV).

and many other troubles. Yet no political, religious, or economic system seems able to offer a workable, lasting solution.

Our world has seen wonderful advances in technology, medicine, and other fields that improve our lives in various ways. But many people wonder how long we will be around to enjoy them. We continually see news headlines reporting on the latest natural disaster or social catastrophe. Consider the number of movies that have been produced in the last few years depicting the end of the world through war, disease, a poisoned environment, or other kinds of disasters. Several films have also been made about people who were left to survive alone under harsh conditions in the natural world or in space. Our society seems to be asking, "Will our world make it?" "Will we be left alone without hope?"

Can we have peace and purpose in a world that seems to be falling apart?

What About God?

We wonder if it is possible for us to have peace, purpose, and empowerment in a world that seems to be falling apart with each passing day. The circumstances in our world lead many people to wrestle with basic questions about their own existence, such as "Why am I here?" and "What is the meaning of my life?" It also makes them wonder about the existence of a Higher Being to whom they might appeal for help. Yet many people, especially in Western societies, find it hard to believe in the reality of anything "spiritual" or "supernatural." They have been trained to question the authenticity of anything that goes beyond the scientific method, beyond what can be seen and heard by their five senses or explained by their intellect. Many people are also tired of hearing about religion, because it hasn't proven to supply answers to their questions or power for overcoming their difficulties. They want something relevant, something authentic, that they can hold on to. But the religions they have grown up with or have observed in their society seem disconnected from their daily desires, hopes, needs, hurts, and troubles.

People are wrestling with questions such as "Why am I here?" and "What is the meaning of my life?"

If there is a God, what is He like? Some people picture God as an old man with a white beard who sits on a throne in heaven and is always ready to punish people for their mistakes. Other people imagine God as a "force" that permeates the universe. Still others depict God through various images that resemble people or animals. But regardless of their concept of God, they often see Him as a distant Being who does not understand what it means to be a human struggling to live on this earth.

Yet, what Jesus Christ taught about God was entirely different from these depictions. He made some remarkable statements about God's vital connection to human beings as our Creator and "Father," about His presence among us, and about His concern for our hurts and suffering. Far from being distant, He did something extraordinary in order to live among us on earth: He became a Man in the person of Jesus Christ—the Son of God—showing us firsthand what He is really like, what He desires for us, and how we can have abundant life. Jesus said that if you have seen Him, you have seen God.[4] And this was His stated mission on earth:

> The Spirit of the LORD is upon Me, because He has anointed Me to preach the gospel to the poor; He has sent

---

[4] See John 14:9.

Me to heal the brokenhearted, to proclaim liberty to the captives and recovery of sight to the blind, to set at liberty those who are oppressed.[5]

Jesus referred to Himself as the "light of the world,"[6] the "bread of life,"[7] and the "good shepherd [who] gives His life for the sheep."[8] As He demonstrated the nature and power of God, He taught us answers to questions such as these:

+ What is truth?

+ What is the meaning of life?

+ What is love?

+ What is my purpose?

Jesus Christ is the source of salvation, hope, and life for humanity. "Following" Him is not the same as following another religion or philosophy. Through Him, we gain entrance to the "kingdom of God"—the fullness of life as it was meant to be lived. Jesus extends the same invitations to us today—to come to Him, to follow Him, to experience rest from our burdens, to discover renewed purpose, and to find true peace.

Answering Jesus' Invitation

In this book, we will look at the life and teachings of Jesus Christ. And we will be introduced to contemporary people from various backgrounds who will tell the story of how and why they have come to believe in Him. The following are two such stories.

Douglas Camarillo has master's degrees in marketing/publicity and public relations. He is a radio host, journalist, and pastor. He responded to the invitation of Jesus when his relationship with

---

[5] Luke 4:18.
[6] John 8:12; 9:5.
[7] John 6:35, 48; see also verses 33, 51.
[8] John 10:11.

his wife deteriorated, and Jesus healed his marriage and gave him peace. "I came from a dysfunctional home where my parents were divorced when I was twelve years old. (My future stepmother was our maid.) With my father's support, I continued with my studies and graduated with excellent grades. At a young age, I was promoted to higher positions, and, at age twenty-five, I became a member of a group of executives of a very important chain of radio and television stations in my home country of Venezuela. Life was fast-paced, and I was earning good money and living without limits. It was a sparkling world: There were constant parties, work meetings, and social events with available alcohol and women. It was, in truth, an accelerated and without-limits lifestyle.

"When I was thirty-one, I met my wife, Nena. She was working for the competing television station. We got married and moved to Miami, Florida, where I wanted to continue working in the media and live a similar lifestyle. I worked in several places, but, in the meantime, my marriage was falling apart. My wife and I would fight over which one of us was in charge, or who could step on the other person and be superior. Pride was wreaking havoc in our relationship, and I considered leaving my wife. However, with our marriage in pieces, we visited King Jesus Church, and Jesus came and radically changed our lives for the better. He restored our marriage, crushed our pride, and ended the anger, the fighting, and the arguments in our home. He put all things in order, and we learned what our individual places were in our marriage. We received counseling and inner healing, and God's reordering of our lives brought us peace. We have now been married for nineteen years and are more in love and happier than on our wedding day. Of course, we experience the normal adjustments and changes that come with married life, but with blessing and tranquility."

Renee Khobragade is a young teacher who has master's degrees in literature and educational leadership. She responded to Jesus' invitation to come to Him and find rest when her life was full of turmoil.

"I was born in Latin America and raised in a strict, dysfunctional home. My uncle abused me when I was four years old; later, other people did the same for several more years. This caused me to experience frustration, fear, and anger, because I knew that I could never say anything to my parents about those incidents. Furthermore, I grew to hate my mother because she would make me feel unworthy and condemned by God. In our home, verbal and physical abuse was the norm, and my parents fought constantly. When I was twenty, my father died, and that event pushed me to the emotional edge. I started to visit clubs, to fight, and to go from one relationship to another, trying to fill the void within me. One day, during a fight with my mother, I threatened to kill her, and she put a restraining order on me. I had to leave home, and this was when my family hit rock bottom.

"A series of events took place that year, until, one day, when I was on my way to the airport, a friend offered to lead me in the prayer of salvation to accept Jesus into my heart. I don't know why, but the tears began to flow uncontrollably. As I repeated the prayer, I could feel the peace of God flooding me, and I realized that I had finally found what I had been desperately seeking for years. Jesus Christ saved me. He pulled me out of the pit, thanks to His work on the cross. He healed, delivered, transformed, and restored my life, as well as the relationships that I had destroyed with my anger and bitterness. I can honestly say that I am a new creature in Christ and that He has given me my righteous identity. Today I can experience His love, joy, peace, and prosperity."

Why believe in Jesus? He invites you to come to Him and receive the abundant life He desires for you, just as these two individuals did.

2

What Is Truth?

P eople have been searching for truth for as long as the human race has existed. Some men and women have spent their entire lives in this quest. The science of logic, the numerous world religions, the many philosophical theories of life, and the branches of natural and social science, such as biology, physics, chemistry, psychology, sociology, and cultural anthropology—all these reflect the human search for truth and meaning.

The Search for Truth

No rational person wants to live according to falsehood, deceit, or lies. Everyone wants to know the truth. And the most important truths we can discover relate to our origin and purpose as human beings, answering such questions as "Who are we?" and "Why do we exist?" Yet, with so many ideas about truth circulating in our world, where do we begin such a quest? If there is truth, how do we find it? These questions are more difficult for us to address today than they were at other times in history because we're living in an era that encourages a relativistic view of life.

For example, many people believe that it is legitimate to say, "Yes, this is true" in only a limited way in a specific situation; they don't believe there is a truth that can apply universally. Many of our schools and universities teach that there are no absolute truths, that all truths are relative and conditional. The idea is promoted that what is true for people in the United States may not be true for people in China or Argentina or Lithuania or Ethiopia or another country. Additionally, what is true today may not be true tomorrow, and every scientific assumption or theory is subject to revision based on new information.

Due to this pervasive mind-set, most people seek out temporary truths, or what's true for them at a given moment. Additionally, the worries of life distract the majority of us from seeking an answer to the transcendent question of whether there is any ultimate, universal truth. Instead, we seek theories and advice that can just help us get through another day. Although this type of information doesn't answer our deepest longings and questions about life, we often feel it is the best we can do.

Of those who do engage in an active search for truth, many explore the realms of abstract theory, scientific inquiry, theology, religion, psychology, and philosophy. However, their search often becomes endlessly cyclical. New questions arise, so they add more uncertainty to their knowledge. This results in a lack of satisfaction and a sense that they will never be able to attain ultimate truth.

Yet, if we could discover *the* truth, it would provide the answers to our deepest questions, as well as to our everyday needs. To know ultimate truth would be to enter the highest level of reality and learn what that truth means for us.

Truth is the highest level of reality.

Jesus Said He Is the Truth

Jesus once had a fascinating discussion with a man named Pilate who, at the time, was the Roman governor of Judea. Their dialogue transcends history because it deals with the question of ultimate truth. The discussion becomes even more potent when we realize that it took place as Jesus was on trial for His life after being accused of sedition against Rome. Here is a portion of their exchange:

> Jesus answered, "My kingdom is not of this world. If My kingdom were of this world, My servants would fight, so that I should not be delivered to the Jews; but now My kingdom is not from here." Pilate therefore said to Him, "Are You a king then?" Jesus answered, "You say rightly that I am a king. For this cause I was born, and for this cause I have come into the world, that I should bear witness to the truth. Everyone who is of the truth hears My voice." Pilate said to Him, "*What is truth?*"[9]

Jesus did not respond to Pilate's last question, even though Jesus had previously told His followers, "I am the way, the truth, and the life. No one comes to the Father except through Me."[10] With this statement, Jesus was indicating, "If you are confused and lost, and don't know in what direction to go, 'I am the way.' If you are looking for someone in whom to trust, something to believe in, or wisdom for what you should do, 'I am...the truth.' If you are seeking an answer to why you exist and how you should live, 'I am the life.'"

It's not clear whether or not Pilate spoke the words "*What is truth?*" in his native language of Latin. If so, he would have said, "Quid est veritas?" It is interesting to note that the fourteen letters that make up that sentence are an anagram—they can be switched around to form another phrase in Latin, "Est vir qui adest," which means "It is the man who is here."[11]

---

9 John 18:36–38.
10 John 14:6.
11 *The Columbia Electronic Encyclopedia*, 6th ed. (Columbia University Press, 2012). All rights reserved.

The point is that truth could be found in the Man who was standing right in front of Pilate—in the person of Jesus Christ. The truth of Jesus is not abstract, relative, or ideological. It is definite, consistent, and universally applicable. Such an assertion is foreign to many people's reason and prior experience. How can one person define what truth is, much less embody it?

Truth is not abstract or ideological; it is found in the person of Jesus Christ.

Jesus Spoke the Truth

The theme of truth is central to Jesus' teachings. In fact, all through the written record of His life and sayings, He began many of His statements with the phrase "Assuredly, I say to you…"; or, as another Bible translation puts it, "I tell you the truth…."[12] He wanted there to be no doubt in the minds of His hearers that what He was saying was unequivocally real. Jesus' disciple John described Him as "full of grace and truth."[13] He is completely trustworthy. Here are a few examples of Jesus' sayings:

> Most assuredly, I say to you, unless one is born again, he cannot see the kingdom of God.[14]

> Most assuredly, I say to you, he who believes in Me has everlasting life.[15]

> Assuredly, I say to you, whoever does not receive the kingdom of God as a little child will by no means enter it.[16]

---

[12] NIV.
[13] John 1:14.
[14] John 3:3.
[15] John 6:47.
[16] Luke 18:17.

In other statements, Jesus declared that God's Word is truth.[17] He associated the truth with being in the light,[18] where there is nothing deceitful or vague; rather, all is plainly seen, done, and said. He declared that knowing the truth is the pathway to personal freedom.[19] He questioned those who opposed Him because they did not believe the truth.[20]

How Is Jesus the Truth?

Even though Jesus always *spoke* the truth, on what basis could He make the claim "I *am*...the truth"? I would like to present two main reasons.

1. In Him Is Life

The Scriptures refer to Jesus as *"the Word"* who became flesh:

In the beginning was the Word, and *the Word was with God, and the Word was God.* He was in the beginning with God. All things were made through Him, and without Him nothing was made that was made. *In Him was life,* and the life was the light of men....And the Word became flesh and dwelt among us.[21]

Jesus was not just a prophet, a great teacher, or an exceptional man. He was God in the flesh—fully God and fully man. He was divine, as well as human. There has never been, nor will there ever be, anyone else like Him in the history of the world. He came for a specific, crucial purpose:

---

[17] John 17:17
[18] John 3:21
[19] John 8:32.
[20] See John 8:40–46.
[21] John 1:1–4, 14.

> For God so loved the world that He gave His only begotten Son, that whoever believes in Him should not perish but have everlasting life. For God did not send His Son into the world to condemn the world, but that the world through Him might be saved.[22]

God is manifested in three Persons—God the Father, God the Son, and God the Holy Spirit. This fact is reflected in the following statement from Scripture: "The grace of the Lord Jesus Christ, and the love of God, and the communion of the Holy Spirit be with you all."[23] Father, Son (Jesus, or the "Word"), and Holy Spirit make up the triune deity, or the Trinity. They are three Persons of the same essence. As God, Jesus is ultimate Reality, or Truth.

Jesus was born on this earth as a human being to reveal the truth of who God is, and of who we are in Him; to die on the cross, taking the punishment for our rebellion against God (sin); to bring us back to Himself; and to give us everlasting, abundant life. "We know that the Son of God has come and has given us an understanding, that we may know Him who is true; and we are in Him who is true, in His Son Jesus Christ. This is the true God and eternal life."[24]

Jesus came to reveal the truth of who God is, and of who we are in Him.

What does the name "Jesus" signify? We read in the Scriptures, "And you shall call His name Jesus, for He will save His people from their sins."[25] The Hebrew word for Jesus is *Yeshua*, which means "Jehovah [God] is salvation." Jesus came to us as the Savior

---

[22] John 3:16–17.
[23] 2 Corinthians 13:14.
[24] 1 John 5:20.
[25] Matthew 1:21.

of the world. Therefore, the name by which He is most widely known expresses the true essence of His nature, and it defines the purpose of His life on earth.

Jesus Is the Way to Ultimate Truth

The second reason Jesus could say, "I am...the truth" is that we can be reconciled to God our Father only through Him. He is the only path to knowing and receiving ultimate Truth. He came to demonstrate the words and ways of God to us, so that we would receive them and return to Him. Jesus said, "Do you not believe that I am in the Father, and the Father in Me? The words that I speak to you I do not speak on My own authority; but the Father who dwells in Me does the works."[26] Jesus' mission was to bring God's words, or truth, to humanity. His teachings and actions revealed this truth, so that we could be set free. "Therefore if the Son makes you free, you shall be free indeed."[27]

Acknowledging and Receiving the Truth

The declarations that Jesus is the Truth and that He was God in the flesh are too much for some people to accept today. Consequently, they may reject Him or criticize or denounce His followers. The same was true of many religious leaders in Jesus' day. They even wanted to kill Jesus for what He taught and for the actions He took—including healing people and performing other miracles. Jesus told them, "You seek to kill Me, because My word has no place in you."[28]

Even though they sought to kill Him, they could never find any legitimate reason for indicting Him. He was always consistent in who He was, what He said, and what He did. He spoke the truth at

---

[26] John 14:10.
[27] John 8:36.
[28] John 8:37.

all times, and He continually showed compassion to those who were sick and despairing. The only way the religious leaders were able to have Him condemned to death was to bring phony charges of sedition against Him.

Jesus was born with the purpose of testifying to the truth.

Let us return to the dialogue between Jesus and Pilate, when the governor asked, "What is truth?" Again, the Truth was standing before him in the person of Jesus Christ. For the first time in his life, the Roman leader was confronted with ultimate Truth but was unaware of it. Ironically, it was Pilate's job to determine the truth of whether or not Jesus was guilty.

Why had Pilate asked Jesus "What is truth?" Apparently, it was not because he believed ultimate truth could really be discovered. Perhaps he was being skeptical or evasive. In the end, Pilate did not uphold the truth but allowed an innocent Man to die. Pilate had previously declared, "I find no fault in Him [Jesus] at all."[29] After talking with Jesus, the governor knew that He was not guilty of rebellion against Rome and that He was being falsely accused. Jesus had even stated previously, "My kingdom is not of this world." However, the Roman leader succumbed to the demand of the inflamed crowd that Jesus be put to death. "When Pilate saw that he could not prevail at all, but rather that a tumult was rising, he took water and washed his hands before the multitude, saying, 'I am innocent of the blood of this just Person. You see to it.'"[30]

---

[29] John 18:38.
[30] Matthew 27:24.

"Washing our hands" of the truth does not take away our responsibility when we stand before the Truth. There is only one way in which we should respond: by acknowledging and receiving Him.

Each of Jesus' words and promises will come to pass. Our human understanding is partial and conditional. Challenging or going against Jesus' teachings and declarations turns us into opponents of the Truth; and, sooner or later, we will suffer the consequences of rejecting Him. Yet, if we accept Him as the Truth—if we believe in Him—we will receive forgiveness, peace, and spiritual understanding.

The only way to find the Truth is to receive Him.

What is the process by which we receive Jesus as the Truth? It does not happen through our human logic or reason alone, or through our natural senses. It comes through "revelation"—through acknowledging and accepting the truth of who Jesus is, and what He has said and done—and by putting our trust and belief in Him. This is what it means to have faith.

Let us briefly compare reason and faith. When we reason with our intellect, we seek to understand something before we believe it, accept it, and act on it. This is a valid process to employ in relation to the realities and properties of our physical world. It is not my intent to suggest that we eliminate reason but rather that we assign it its appropriate place and use.

In contrast, when we exercise faith, we receive spiritual truth by first believing what God has said; this leads us to be able to understand that spiritual truth with our minds and to apply it to our lives. For example, the Bible says, "By faith we understand that the worlds were framed by the word of God, so that the things which are seen were not made of things which are visible."[31] Reason cannot be the first resource we draw upon when dealing with subjects that transcend the natural world because, in the world of the supernatural, only faith and spiritual discernment will enable us to receive revelation that can afterward be applied to the natural world by way of our reason.

I want to make clear that I am not diminishing the importance of the intellect or education. I am pro-intellect and pro-education. I have both a master's degree and a doctorate in theology, and I encourage young people to attend college and professional school. But I believe that if we submit our faculties of reason and logic to God, He will make them creative and powerful with spiritual understanding.

The following is the story of John Laffitte, who was trained as an aerospace engineer. After discovering the truth in Jesus Christ, he committed his intellect and reason to the glory of God. The truth of Jesus releases a supernatural power to save, restore, heal, set free, and give life. Though some people dismiss supernatural manifestations from God when they witness them, others, like John, acknowledge that there is more to life than what can be known by the physical senses.

"From the time I was a child, I had a strong desire to be an astronaut. In my pursuit of this goal, I attended MIT (Massachusetts Institute of Technology) and later the University of Michigan in Ann Arbor, where I earned a doctorate in aerospace engineering. During my years as a university student, my mother found Christ, and each time I visited her on vacation, she would take me to church. That is how I obtained an intellectual knowledge of God, but I still lived as I thought fit.

"On my way to graduation, all I can say is that Jesus revealed Himself to me as the living Christ that He is. In 1992, I began to experience a deep hunger for Him. While I watched a Christian

---

[31] Hebrews 11:3.

preacher on television, I knelt down and made Jesus my Lord and Savior. At that moment, I became a different person. I would pray for hours, read the Bible tirelessly, and attend every event I could at my local church. I submerged myself in His things! God placed a call on my life to become a teacher for the body of Christ, as described in Ephesians 4:11.

"While my application to become an astronaut was being processed by NASA, I taught as an associate professor at the University of Miami and worked as an engineering consultant. Later, I obtained my doctorate and worked as a researcher at Florida International University, where I conducted research for NASA, the FAA (Federal Aviation Administration), the DOE (Department of Energy), and other agencies. However, I noticed that God kept pulling me more each day toward the ministry. My gift in teaching His Word was recognized by others whenever I taught. The moment came when I had to decide between my desire to be an astronaut and my calling to serve God as a Bible teacher. I struggled greatly, until I decided to do the will of God.

"As a result, today, I am a minister of Jesus Christ in one of the largest Hispanic churches in America, a teacher to the body of Christ, and executive vice president of SMU (Supernatural Ministry University, an educational institution affiliated with King Jesus International Ministry). The purpose of SMU is to change the lives of thousands of Christians by activating them in the supernatural power of God. I feel complete when I see that God uses me to heal and deliver people in a supernatural way, as well as to train them in a comprehensive knowledge of His Word, the Bible. I have witnessed how He opens the eyes of the blind and the ears of the deaf; how He lengthens short legs, creates new organs and other body parts, and raises people out of their wheelchairs.

"I have come to understand that I am not an engineer who knows the Word of God. I am a minister of Jesus Christ who has a knowledge of engineering."

First faith perceives; then reason applies.

Reconnecting to Ultimate Truth

If Jesus could reveal Himself to the scientific mind of an engineer who formerly accepted only what his five natural senses could perceive, He can do the same for you. Perhaps you have been trained to consider the world through empirical facts alone, but you know that something is missing in your life. There is a void you cannot fill, philosophical questions you have not been able to answer, or sicknesses you have not been able to overcome. Even more than other people who do not have a scientific inclination, you know there is a limit to what your mind can know and interpret in life.

Regardless of how intelligent you are or how much education you have, you are still a human being whose spirit needs to connect to its Source—the ultimate Truth, Jesus Christ. Open up your heart and allow Him to reveal Himself to you. In Him, you will find answers to life that all the scientific knowledge put together could never attain.

For example, once, when I gave a teaching on the power of Jesus to transform lives and heal any sickness, an amazing miracle took place. After receiving a blood transfusion during surgery, a forty-year-old woman had been diagnosed with hepatitis C—an infectious disease that causes patients to suffer a chronic condition that can progress into cirrhosis of the liver and cancer. This woman's doctor is a leader in my church, and he had invited her to the service. When she heard the teaching, she decided to accept Jesus as her Savior. Later, I began to demonstrate the truth that I had taught, praying against any sickness that the people in the congregation might be afflicted with.

I had never met this woman, and I wasn't aware of what was wrong with her. However, the power of Jesus came upon her; she later told us that she felt an indescribable "fire" course through her body. The next day, her doctor examined her and ran new tests to verify her healing. To her surprise, all of the tests came back negative! God had done a work in her hepatic cells, eradicating the viral infection completely. The word that I preached was not just theory, because Jesus has the power to do miracles, and He said that if we would believe in Him, *"all things are possible."*[32]

How Will You Respond?

If you have looked for the truth everywhere you could think of, without success, it could be that you were looking in the wrong place, knocking on the wrong door, inquiring of someone who didn't know, or asking someone who didn't have anything to give. Today, I present Jesus to you as the Truth and the answer to all of your questions. He is the only One who can truly satisfy your thirst—for genuine love, for justice, for fulfillment, and for anything else you could ever need. When you believe in Jesus and receive Him, He will give you the peace that has eluded you, the love that has been withheld from you, and the hope that has been denied you.

Jesus Christ, the Truth, stands before you now. How will you respond? Will you turn your back on Him? Will you seek another truth that seems easier or more convenient? Will you "wash your hands" of ultimate reality? Or will you humble yourself before God, acknowledging that Jesus is His Son and that He died for your sins and your sickness? It would be a sad state of affairs to

---

[32] See, for example, Mark 9:23.

believe in a lie and then realize the truth when it is too late. Have courage and face the truth of Christ, recognizing that you need His lordship and salvation.

God's Holy Spirit reveals the truth to us and gives us an opportunity to respond to it. Jesus said, "For this cause I have come into the world, that I should bear witness to the truth. Everyone who is of the truth hears My voice."[33] The Bible tells us that God has given each of us a measure of faith.[34] Therefore, respond to Jesus by telling Him, "By the faith I have been given, I receive You as the way, the truth, and the life—my Savior."

Why believe in Jesus? He is the Truth.

When we stand before the Truth, our response will determine our destiny.

---

[33] John 18:37.
[34] See Romans 12:3.

3

Religion or Relationship?

Multitudes of people throughout the world belong to a particular religion or subscribe to certain religious beliefs. People often participate in religious activities because they have a heartfelt desire for significance, guidance, and comfort in life. Although some people do not believe in the existence of a Higher Being, or do not support any form of religion, most people who hold religious beliefs realize that there is a spiritual aspect to their lives. They understand that there is more to life than what can be known by their physical senses.

A religion may be defined as a belief system relating to ultimate reality and the meaning of life. It often includes rituals, rules, and guidelines for how to live. In some countries, multiple religions are practiced by the populace, each religion having specific beliefs, prescribed behavior patterns, liturgies, and so forth. Religion deals with such concepts as the existence and nature of a Higher Being (God or gods), life and death, good and evil, moral and immoral behavior (sin) and their consequences, the afterlife, the supernatural, sacred writings, and theology.

Can a Religion Be Separated from Its Founder?

Generally, a religion is established on the beliefs and works of its founder. However, if we were to remove the person who founded the belief system from the subsequent religion, the religion could still exist and function. For example, a person can be a Buddhist without Buddha or a Muslim without Muhammad. Both of these religious founders died centuries ago, and they do not need to be present for people to follow their particular philosophies and ideas.

Many people consider Jesus to be the founder of a religion—Christianity. Numerous people, to a greater or lesser extent, believe in and follow His teachings. They may belong to a denomination or church that comes under the religious category called "Christianity." But Jesus' purpose in coming to earth was not to establish a "religion"; neither did He intend merely to add His teachings to the beliefs of other religions. Instead, He came to offer *Himself* as our Savior. Consequently, if we were to take away Jesus Christ from Christianity, it would cease to exist as a reality. Without the living Jesus, what is left is only a "religion" called Christianity, which is just a semblance of that reality.

True Christianity does not consist in merely agreeing with or following Jesus' teachings and example. Of course, following His general teachings and example can bring some benefit to people's lives, but it is not enough to transform them from the inside out; it is not enough to address their fundamental problems and needs; and it is not enough to be eternally effective. Only a relationship with Jesus can fulfill these needs.

Without the living Jesus, Christianity is only a semblance of reality.

Believing in Jesus Is Not the Same as Joining a Religion

No religion can ultimately satisfy the human need for meaning, guidance, and comfort, because religion goes only so far. Let us explore various ways in which believing in Jesus is different from belonging to or following a religion.

1. Religious Founders Were Human Beings, but Jesus Was God in the Flesh

Generally, the founders of the various religions were men and women who believed they had received some type of spiritual enlightenment or philosophical insights. Although some of their followers may have later claimed that their leaders were divine, the majority of those founders did not make that claim themselves. But Jesus clearly affirmed that He is God. Though He never sought people's worship, He accepted it because it rightly belonged to Him.

> Then those who were in the boat came and worshipped [Jesus], saying, "Truly You are the Son of God."[35]

> Then, as [Jesus] was now drawing near the descent of the Mount of Olives, the whole multitude of the disciples began to rejoice and praise God with a loud voice for all the mighty works they had seen, saying: "'Blessed is the King who comes in the name of the LORD!' Peace in heaven and glory in the highest!" And some of the Pharisees called to Him from the crowd, "Teacher, rebuke Your disciples." But He answered and said to them, "I tell you that if these should keep silent, the stones would immediately cry out."[36]

Jesus was not just a prophet, a great teacher, or an exceptional man. He was God in the flesh. Therefore, a central difference between Jesus and every other founder of a religion is that the latter were mere human beings, but Jesus was—and is—divine.

---

[35] Matthew 14:33.
[36] Luke 19:37–40.

2. Religious Founders Are Dead and Buried, but Jesus Was Raised from the Dead

The founders of the various religions that people follow today are dead, or they will die. Yet genuine belief in Jesus Christ is based not just on Jesus as a teacher who lived two thousand years ago but on the *living* person of Jesus. It depends on the fact that after Jesus was put to death on a Roman cross, He was raised from the dead and is still alive today. Those who have received Jesus acknowledge that after He paid the price to deliver all people from spiritual, physical, mental, and emotional oppression, He conquered death and was resurrected before returning to God the Father in heaven. Jesus is able to give us eternal life because He *is* life, and because He defeated death forever. And, whoever receives Him will also one day be physically resurrected to live with Him eternally. We read in the Scriptures:

> But now Christ is risen from the dead, and has become the firstfruits of those who have fallen asleep [died]. For since by man came death, by Man also came the resurrection of the dead. For as in Adam all die, even so in Christ all shall be made alive.[37]

No other belief system or religion requires that its followers believe in the resurrection of its founder. In addition, none other is founded on the fact that the leader surrendered His life on behalf of His followers, even before they knew Him or made a decision to believe in Him and accept His love and sacrifice.

When a person receives the resurrected Jesus, he enters into a personal relationship with Him. Then, he begins to understand and follow Jesus' teachings in ways he never could before, because he has experienced an inner transformation that includes a new

---

[37] 1 Corinthians 15:20–22.

nature and the gift of God's own Spirit dwelling within him. When the believer follows Jesus' teachings and obeys His commandments, it is a reflection of his devotion to Him, not the result of mere religious duty.[38]

As we have noted, some people who lack a vital relationship with Jesus endeavor to follow His teachings. They may call themselves "Christian," and they may belong to a church or denomination designated as "Christian." They may desire to love God and help other people. However, the essential element of a connection with the living Jesus is missing from their lives. They simply accept certain teachings, ideas, and traditions connected with Jesus, or they follow a system of moral principles and laws. Consequently, they are, in effect, involved in a religion that, while it contains some good aspects, does not manifest the reality and power of true Christianity.

Numerous people are in this condition today. Their situation can be described by the following statement from a biblical writer:

"Having a form of godliness but denying its power."[39] This does not necessarily mean that they knowingly or actively deny the power of Christ—they might be dismayed at that idea. However, it does mean that they lack the life, power, and presence of Jesus within them. They have only the appearance of genuine faith while they actually live according to outward rituals or principles.

When someone believes in the living Jesus, he does not just accept His teachings—he enters into a personal relationship with Him.

---

[38] See, for example, John 14:15, 23–24.
[39] 2 Timothy 3:5.

Unfortunately, if the living person of Jesus were to be removed from many people who profess to believe in Him, it would not alter how they conduct their daily lives. This is because they aren't actively relying on His presence, help, and power, much less on His sacrifice on the cross to reconcile them to God. To them, following Christ usually means going to religious services and following certain customs. They may try to observe various rules and regulations, striving to be good enough for God through their own efforts and by doing charitable acts. They don't realize that they are substituting religion for vital faith in Jesus.

Many people who follow a religion engage in various good works, and such deeds are commendable. All of us must help other people who are poor, hurting, and destitute. In fact, Jesus explained that if we truly believe in Him, we will help other people, and it will be just as if we are helping Him. He stated,

> I was hungry and you gave Me food; I was thirsty and you gave Me drink; I was a stranger and you took Me in; I was naked and you clothed Me; I was sick and you visited Me; I was in prison and you came to Me....Assuredly, I say to you, inasmuch as you did it to one of the least of these My brethren, you did it to Me.[40]

However, no matter how many good works we may do, these acts are inadequate in themselves to reconcile us to God and to enable us to have a true relationship with Him. For example, they can never make amends for our sins, or the wrong things we have said and done. Only a sinless Sacrifice could do that. Jesus had a sinless nature, and He never sinned; therefore, He was able to pay that price for us on the cross. And only when we accept His sacrifice on our behalf can we be reconciled to God.

---

[40] Matthew 25:35–36, 40.

In addition, doing good deeds cannot earn us eternal life. We are granted eternal life by God when we believe in and receive Jesus, who, as we have seen, is "the way, the truth, and the life."[41] Moreover, good works will not give us the ability to solve our deepest human needs or our "impossible" situations—such as entrenched problems and incurable illnesses. The resurrected Jesus alone can overcome those through His supernatural power.

Joshua López has a master's degree in choreography and is a master chef. He found himself in an "impossible" situation, and his life is a testimony to the compassion and power of the living Jesus:

"I grew up knowing the gospel. However, at the age of twelve, I left the way of the Lord because I could not understand why God did not heal me of dyslexia or protect me from being sexually abused. I became involved in prostitution, worked as a stripper in bars, got involved in satanic pacts, and even tried different religions. After trying everything, I ended up not believing in good or evil. In 1982, I overdosed on drugs, and I saw my spirit separate from my body. I cried out to God, telling Him that if He set me free, I would serve Him for the rest of my life. At that moment, I felt my spirit return to my body, even though I was left catatonic for several hours, and those around me thought I was dead. In my unconscious state, I perceived that a 'fire' from God had fallen on me, giving me the conviction that I was free from crack and heroin.

"I searched for God in my own way but soon returned to prostitution and separated myself from those who believed in Him. Sometime later, tests revealed that I had AIDS, and I was given six months to live. I suffered pain, black spots on my skin, and fatigue that made walking very difficult. I looked for God in prayer without going to a church or telling anyone what was happening to me."Six months later, I was still alive, and I began to attend a church. I stayed for four years and grew spiritually, until the day

---

[41] John 14:6.

the Lord sent me to King Jesus Ministry. There, I found my identity in Christ and received deliverance in the areas of addiction, sexual abuse, rejection, spiritual captivity, and more. When I had lost hope of ever getting married, God blessed me with a wife, and we have been married for several years and have two beautiful daughters. My wife is a faith-filled woman who always believed in my healing, which was progressive, just like my faith was. I thank God for His faithfulness and love, for my family, and for my pastors, who always believed in me."

The power of the living Jesus still saves, heals, and delivers people in nations across the globe today, because He was raised from the dead and continues to minister to us. He is alive!

The resurrected Jesus alone can overcome entrenched problems and incurable diseases through His supernatural power.

---

3. Religious Founders Are No Longer Present with Their Followers on Earth, but Jesus Is with His Followers

Again, the founders of the various religions are dead, or they will die. After death, they have no contact with their followers. Yet Jesus made this promise to those who receive Him, regardless of what century of human history they may live in: "I am with you always, even to the end of the age."[42]

How does Jesus continue to be with His followers, even today? He said that He would live *within* them: "I will not leave you orphans; I will come to you....If anyone loves Me, he will keep My word; and My Father will love him, and We will come to him

---

[42] Matthew 28:20.

and make Our home with him."[43] Jesus also promised that the
very Spirit of God would dwell in those who believe, to be their
Counselor, or Helper: "And I will pray the Father, and He will
give you another Helper, that He may abide with you forever—
the Spirit of truth."[44]

Therefore, Father, Son, and Spirit—the triune God—reside
within us when we believe in Jesus and receive Him as our Savior
and Lord. This reality gives us access to the spiritual realm in
which God says all our needs will be supplied and all things are
possible.[45] Again, Jesus continues to heal and do miracles today in
the lives of those who believe in Him, and He is with them *always*.

4. Followers of Religion "Join"; Followers of Jesus Are Spiritually Reborn

Another difference between the various religious systems and
belief in Jesus is the way in which people join a religion and relate
to the other members of that religion, compared to the way in
which people receive Jesus and become united with Him and with
their fellow believers. Many people become members of a religion
because it is in keeping with their family's heritage or race, and/or
the cultural tradition of the community or nation in which they
live. An individual may become a member of a religion through
various avenues. For example, he may simply be born to parents
who adhere to that belief system; he may go through a ritual of
some sort; or, he may merely state that he wants to become a
member of the religious community.

Sometimes, people feel they have no choice but to join a particular religion—it is expected of them by their family or their society, so they experience pressure to conform. In certain societies,
if a person does not accept the religion of his community, he faces

[43] John 14:18, 23.
[44] John 14:16–17.
[45] See, for example, Philippians 4:19; Mark 9:23.

severe consequences, such as rejection, loss of liberty, and even loss of life. To a certain extent, this explains the force and growth of some religions. But when an individual truly accepts Jesus' invitation to come to Him, that person does not receive Jesus by means of his family background or by his community, cultural, or racial ties. Nor does he do so by mere agreement with Jesus' teachings and principles. And he cannot do so through any external compulsion. Instead, he receives Jesus by spiritual rebirth, an experience that is sometimes called being "born of God" or "born again." The Scriptures say:

> Yet to all who received [Jesus], to those who believed in his name, he gave the right to become children of God— children born not of natural descent, nor of human decision or a husband's will, but born of God.[46]

> [Jesus said,] "Most assuredly, I say to you, unless one is born again, he cannot see the kingdom of God."[47]

We are "born of God," or "born again," when we make a personal commitment to believe in Jesus and to receive Him as the only Lord and sufficient Savior of our lives. Unlike some religions, the will of the individual is essential in this process—although the spiritual rebirth itself is achieved only by God, not the individual.

We do not receive Jesus through our family background or cultural ties, or through mere agreement with His teachings; we receive Him by spiritual rebirth.

Additionally, even though a person may join a particular religion and share common beliefs with the other people who embrace that

---

[46] John 1:12–13 (NIV).
[47] John 3:3.

religion, there is nothing that *intrinsically* connects that person with the others in the group. The same is true of any group whose members all agree on certain ideas and beliefs.

In contrast, when an individual receives Jesus and is born again, he becomes spiritually united with Jesus and all others who have received Him. That individual is related in a deep and eternal way to the other believers—not merely in a social, intellectual, or emotional way. Accordingly, this spiritual association is neither external nor optional. Jesus told His followers regarding their relationship to Him:

> Abide in Me, and I in you. As the branch cannot bear fruit of itself, unless it abides in the vine, neither can you, unless you abide in Me. I am the vine, you are the branches. He who abides in Me, and I in him, bears much fruit; for without Me you can do nothing.[48]

And, regarding believers' relationships with each another, the Scriptures say, "We, being many, are one body in Christ, and individually members of one another."[49] Speaking of His followers, Jesus prayed to God the Father, "That they may be one just as We are one: I in them, and You in Me; that they may be made perfect in one."[50] All who believe in Jesus are united, or "one"—with God and with each other. Jesus referred to those who believe in Him as His "church."[51] This term does not imply an individual church or denomination, or a particular church building, but rather the spiritual unity of Jesus' followers.

---

[48] John 15:4–5.
[49] Romans 12:5.
[50] John 17:22–23.
[51] See Matthew 16:18.

5. Followers of Religion Accept a Belief System; Followers of Jesus Enter a Kingdom

Those who adhere to a particular religion accept the teachings and principles that constitute its belief system. Yet, when we receive Jesus, we do not merely agree with Jesus' teachings and principles. We enter an eternal realm of life called the "kingdom of God." In the previous chapter, we discussed Jesus' exchange with Pilate, during which Jesus said, "My kingdom is not of this world." He was referring to the kingdom of God.

Through Jesus, we gain entrance to God's kingdom—the manifestation of His sovereign, heavenly government on earth. The Greek word for "kingdom" is *basileia*, which means "royalty," "rule," "a realm," or "sovereignty," "royal power." It comes from the root word *basileus*, which relates to the idea of a "foundation of power."

Jesus said, "Unless one is born again, he cannot see the kingdom of God."[52] When we are born again, God's kingdom is established within us, and we can "see" it through spiritual eyes. Jesus said, "The kingdom of God does not come with [external] observation; nor will they say, 'See here!' or 'See there!' For indeed, the kingdom of God is within you."[53] God's kingdom is not a political dominion but a realm of the spirit. It must first dwell within us through God's presence, so that it may then be manifested externally through our lives, and so that we will begin to experience the fullness of life that we were meant to have. This is the difference between following religious principles and experiencing true life.

God's kingdom is not a political dominion but a realm of the spirit.

---

[52] John 3:3.
[53] Luke 17:20–21.

Former major-league baseball player Juan Guzmán believed in God and enjoyed success in his career, but he had a void in his life. Yet, when he surrendered his life to God and entered into the fullness of His kingdom, he experienced a remarkable transformation. Here is his story:

"I was born in the Dominican Republic, in a humble little house that was made of palms and had a dirt floor. I grew up there with my parents and four siblings. Our poverty was so great that the four boys slept in one bed. At thirteen, I decided to leave it all behind to seek a future in baseball. After much effort, I was signed as a professional baseball player, in the position of pitcher. As I was about to leave for the United States, my mother gave me a Bible and told me to read it during difficult times, and reading the Bible became a habit for me.

"One day, I was angry because I had spent four long years in the minor leagues without being called up to the major league, due to my inability to control my pitch. But, in my Bible reading, I learned about the covenant that God made with Abraham,[54] and I decided I would make a covenant with God. I asked the Lord to allow me to play in the major league, and, in exchange, I would serve Him the rest of my life.

"The next day, something had changed within me that I could not explain. I used to be afraid and worry constantly, and yet now I was at peace. When I was given the opportunity to play, I performed so well that I was soon promoted to the major league. I ended up winning ten consecutive games, equaling the record of the best pitchers on my team. I was among the top three candidates for the Cy Young award. I was the first pitcher in the history of baseball to pitch the first ball in a World Series game outside of

---

[54] See, for example, Romans 4:13–25.

the United States. I won two consecutive World Series (in 1992 and 1993 with the Toronto Blue Jays). I made history!

"Years later, God reminded me of my covenant. Although I was financially stable, owning properties, investments, and businesses in the United States, Canada, and my native country, there were areas in my life that were void and that I was unable to fill. I had confessed Jesus as my Lord and Savior many times, when I'd watched preachers on television or attended meetings at the Baseball Chapel, but I had done that just to be in good standing with others. I believed in God and helped the poor and needy; but I was also a womanizer and bound to sexual immorality. I would convince myself that I was okay because I wasn't hurting anyone.

"But then, I decided to clean up my life. I surrendered to the Lord for real, and He began to change me. During the previous years, I had been married to baseball. I had been 100 percent dedicated to the sport. Then I began to pray to God for a wife, someone just right for my life, and He heard my prayer. He also set me free from pornography, depression, idolatry, fear, deception, arrogance, anger, bitterness, and unforgiveness. He changed my character. I have learned to be a mentor, to be a better leader, to have more integrity, and to be more responsible and organized. I have even learned to manage my finances and to care for my children, my wife, and my home. The void in me disappeared, and today I can say that I am happy."

Are You in the Kingdom of God?

God is the Supreme Ruler of the universe, including our world, and He wants us to be active participants in His kingdom, experiencing and spreading it here on earth. "The earth is the LORD's, and all its fullness, the world and those who dwell therein."[55]

---

[55] Psalm 24:1.

The problem with "religious Christianity" (not genuine Christianity) is that people who have experienced it or observed it have been presented with only a "mystical" or historical Christ who is unreachable and does not relate to them personally. As a result, a number of them have become skeptical about God and Jesus, so they cannot experience the life He wants to give them. Many people in our world feel depressed, disoriented, and lost because they can't make sense of their existence. They often despair of having a meaningful and satisfying life, to the point where some of them even decide to commit suicide.

Yet the kingdom of God is an eternal reality that can transform any situation. The kingdom brings everything each human being needs, such as salvation, healing, deliverance, prosperity, and purpose. It is to be experienced today, and it is to be applied to whatever circumstance we are undergoing at this moment.

The religions of the world cannot give us true life because they don't have it to offer. Only Jesus, the One who was resurrected, can give it. Our part is to receive Him into our lives. The following is the story of Sandeep J. Khobragade, a businessman from India who once believed in the Hindu gods. Yet, when he needed a miracle, he found that Jesus alone could provide it.

"When I was fourteen, my uncle introduced me to sexual immorality. This filled me with fear and isolated me from my friends and family. I could not share what had happened with anyone, especially not my parents. I felt trapped and helpless! Time passed, and I couldn't turn away from the immorality, regardless of my efforts. I began to seek a solution by consulting idols and astrologers. I spent three years studying astrology, reading horoscopes, and using astrological rocks, mantras, and rituals, but nothing worked. Astrology provided a diagnosis for the problem but did not offer a solution.

"In the meantime, a crisis in the family business led me to the United States in search of new opportunities. There, Jesus began to reveal Himself through circumstances and people, over and over again. I was a devout Hindu and ran from Christians, but I kept searching for the truth and for a way out. For a year, I prayed to Saibaba [a Hindu god] and didn't get an answer. Then, I came across a childhood friend from India who was a Christian. God used him to reveal Jesus to me. When I recognized that Jesus is the truth and that His love follows me, I began to cry and gave my life to Him. All I know is that when I cried out to God, Jesus appeared. He delivered me from sexual immorality and idol worship. Today, I know that Jesus is the way, the truth, and the life. By His grace, I am blessed and happily married to a wonderful woman, and together we serve Him."

Transformation begins with a personal revelation of Jesus Christ.

Jesus came to earth to change the hearts and lives of human beings. He began by calling disciples, and, one by one, He transformed their heart, their mind-set, and their lifestyle through a personal relationship with Him. He did not make them false promises, and He did not force them to believe. Instead, He was a role model. He demonstrated God's power, justice, grace, and mercy. As His disciples were inspired by His life and teachings, they began to yearn to be like Him. Today, Jesus calls us to be His disciples, too, regardless of who we are or how difficult our life circumstances are. He wants to transform us, so that we can become all that God our Creator meant us to be.

Jesus offers us God's kingdom—not a "religion." He declared to His followers, "Do not fear, little flock, for it is your Father's good pleasure to give you the kingdom,"[56] and "Seek the kingdom of God."[57] He also taught the people, "The time is fulfilled, and the kingdom of God is at hand. Repent, and believe in the gospel."[58]

Have you been merely following the rules and rituals of a religion? Or, do you have a relationship with the living Jesus? He gave His last drop of blood on the cross out of love for humanity, and He calls people to Himself from every nation, race, religion, and social stratum in the world. My dear friend, believing in the living Jesus and receiving Him may be costly to you. Some followers of Jesus have been rejected by their family or persecuted by their community or government. In some cases, it has cost people their lives. Yet there are many followers of various religions who are willing to die for something that has no power to transform them or give them eternal life. Are you willing to suffer or give up your life for what is real and true?

When Saul of Tarsus became a believer in Jesus, he was rejected by many people in his culture. But because his heart and life had been transformed, he was able to state with confidence:

> Even though our outward man is perishing, yet the inward man is being renewed day by day. For our light affliction, which is but for a moment, is working for us a far more exceeding and eternal weight of glory, while we do not look at the things which are seen, but at the things which are not seen. For the things which are seen are temporary, but the things which are not seen are eternal.[59]

Why believe in Jesus? Because He offers you true and eternal life.

---

[56] Luke 12:32.
[57] Luke 12:31.
[58] Mark 1:15.
[59] 2 Corinthians 4:16–18.

The following prayer can help you to find the words to accept Jesus' invitation to come to Him. You don't have to say these exact words. You can say the same thing in your own words, as long as you talk to God with a sincere heart and a desire to live for Him. You are not joining a religion but entering into the kingdom of God and beginning an eternal relationship with the living Jesus.

> Heavenly Father, I believe that Jesus died on the cross for me and that He was raised from the dead. I confess that He is my Savior and Lord. I am sorry for all the wrong things I have thought, said, and done. I turn away from them, so that I can turn toward You and everything You desire for my life. Thank You that You promised to come into my heart and transform me. Thank You that I am now "born from above" and have entered Your kingdom. Please use me to spread Your kingdom in this world. Amen!

Now that you have prayed to receive Jesus, find a group of believers following the living, resurrected Jesus, who still transforms lives, heals, and does miracles today. Ask God to intervene in your situations, and trust Him to bring you healing and deliverance, such as have been experienced by the people whose stories you have read in this book. Read and study the Bible, asking God's Holy Spirit to help you grow in your understanding of what it means to live a life with Jesus that is not "religious" but is filled with His vitality, love, and power!

4

Why Is There Pain and Suffering in the World?

A common question people ask is, "If God is so good and powerful, why is there evil and suffering in the world?" They wonder why we have to endure so many tribulations in life—why God permits people to experience broken homes and drug addictions; accidents, sicknesses, and premature death; rape, slavery, racial conflicts, genocide, war, and other forms of violence; natural disasters like earthquakes, tsunamis, and tornadoes; and human misery such as poverty and starvation.

As members of the human race, we must recognize that the root cause of all the distressing and terrible things that take place in our lives and throughout the world is a problem called "sin" and its far-reaching consequences.

Many people consider the word *sin* to be an outdated religious concept. But what is sin? If it is real, how did it become a part of our world? To answer these questions, we need to explore the origin of humanity.

Humanity's Beginning

Our world was designed to be an expression of our Creator and His character, not to be filled with pain and suffering. When God formed the earth, He first made the physical environment, including the plants, the fish, the birds, and all the other animals, and

He pronounced them "good."[60] Then, He made human beings to be like Him in their very essence: "God created man in His own image; in the image of God He created him; male and female He created them."[61] God did not create sinful people—He made them in *His own image*—as a reflection of His love, goodness, power, trustworthiness, creativity, and other attributes. After creating human beings, God pronounced everything He had made "very good."[62] It was a world without evil.

Human beings were created in God's image.

An essential feature of our creation in God's image is that we are spiritual beings. The Scriptures tell us, "God is Spirit,"[63] and each human being has an eternal spirit. Every person also has a soul (the mind, will, and emotions) and a body, enabling him to interact with the physical world.

Additionally, God granted human beings the freedom of choice—including the ability to choose between right and wrong. Our Creator did not desire "robots" who would automatically do what He wanted. Instead, He desired beings who understood and appreciated His own nature and who, of their own free will, chose to live according to that nature. Furthermore, He created humanity to have spiritual union with Him, producing a deep and close relationship.

The "Fall" of Humanity

At the beginning, the first man and woman lived in harmony with God. But then, exercising self-will, they went against the only

---

[60] See Genesis 1:1–25.
[61] Genesis 1:27.
[62] Genesis 1:31.
[63] John 4:24.

requirement God had given them (a condition established for their own protection and well-being), even though God had warned them the result would be death.[64]

Why did the first human beings choose to defy God? They made the decision after being enticed to do so by God's enemy, Satan, also called the devil, or Lucifer. Satan was a created angelic being. However, because he attempted to usurp God, he was expelled from God's presence, along with the other angelic beings who had joined his rebellion.[65] Desiring to harm God, Satan planted a similar rebellious idea in the minds of the first human beings. He told them that if they ignored God's instructions, they would not die but would "be like God, knowing good and evil."[66] In effect, he was saying that they didn't need God in order to live and thrive.

Disastrously, they succumbed to this suggestion to live independently of God, and they consciously pursued their own agenda. They didn't recognize that their very lives depended on remaining connected with their Creator and His nature. Their choice is often called the "fall" of humanity, because human beings went from a high state of having God's nature and reflecting His image to a low state in which they now had a *sinful nature* and exhibited a distorted image of Him. This altered human state is the origin of evil and pain in our world.

The first human beings had been lied to by Satan. They *did* die as a consequence of disobeying God. First, they experienced spiritual death, in which they were separated from God, including His glory and the fullness of His nature. Second, their bodies slowly began to break down, and they eventually experienced physical death.

---

[64] See Genesis 2:17.

[65] See, for example, Isaiah 14:12–15.

[66] Genesis 3:5.

In addition, through their offspring, they passed on both of these disastrous legacies—spiritual and physical death—to the entire human race. As the Scriptures say: "Through one man sin entered the world, and death through sin, and thus death spread to all men, because all sinned."[67]

Because of sin, our physical bodies are now subject to the limitations of time, aging, and, eventually, death. Moreover, even though our spirits are eternal, they are dead to God, separated from His life—unless they are transformed through faith in Jesus' sacrificial death and resurrection. This is why Jesus said that we must be "born again."[68] Our spirits must be reborn so we can once again reflect God's nature.

What Is Sin?

To sin means to violate the laws and commands of God. It is lawlessness against God's Word. Other terms for sin are *transgression* and *iniquity*. Sin is anything that is not in alignment with our Creator and His ways.

Sin manifests itself in various forms. We see it in people who want to run their own lives, making their own decisions independently of God and His ways, just as the first human beings did. We see it in people who try to "earn" God's approval or gain entrance to heaven on their own terms. We see it in people who actively fight against God's laws and commandments, becoming their own authority and setting their own standards of what is right and wrong. We even see it in people who know what is right yet fail to do it.[69]

---

[67] Romans 5:12.
[68] John 3:3, 7.
[69] See James 4:17.

Sin is not a "religious" term; it is a violation of God's laws, Word, and will.

In His Word, God gives us many examples of sin, including "a proud look, a lying tongue, hands that shed innocent blood, a heart that devises wicked plans, feet that are swift in running to evil, a false witness who speaks lies, and one who sows discord among brethren."[70] Some behavior that God calls sin might seem normal and legitimate to us if it is acceptable in our society. However, that does not change how God feels about it, and it does not alter our accountability for it.

If we want to be in God's kingdom, we must reflect the nature of God Himself. That is why the Scripture says, for example:

> Do not be deceived: Neither the sexually immoral [those engaging in intimate relations before marriage] nor idolaters [those giving the place God deserves to another person, being, object, or activity] nor adulterers nor male prostitutes nor homosexual offenders nor thieves nor the greedy nor drunkards nor slanderers nor swindlers will inherit the kingdom of God.[71]

The Scriptures list other corrupt behavior committed by people due to their sinful nature, including "witchcraft; hatred, discord, jealousy, fits of rage, selfish ambition, dissensions, factions and envy; drunkenness, orgies, and the like."[72] When people have not received Jesus, they are estranged from God, so they do not understand His ways. For this reason, they constantly fall into error and neglect to do what is right and good, which would bring peace to their lives. Continuing to violate God's nature keeps people

---

[70] Proverbs 6:17–19.
[71] 1 Corinthians 6:9–10 (NIV).
[72] Galatians 5:20–21 (NIV).

separated from Him, and such separation will always result in spiritual and physical death. "When [wrong] desire has conceived, it gives birth to sin; and sin, when it is full-grown, brings forth death."[73] There is no sin that, continuously practiced, doesn't result in death. Regardless of how people categorize sin, if they don't turn their backs on it, their end will undoubtedly be disastrous.

Every Human Is Born with a Sinful Nature

Some people believe that because they do not commit "major" sins, they are good people who should not be classified as "sinners." Yet the Bible states, "For *all* have sinned and fall short of the glory of God."[74] The sinful nature is present in every human being; we were born with it, having inherited it through humanity's fall. So, sin is something that afflicts all of us, without exception. And sin isn't limited to extreme acts, such as engaging in blatant and repeated immorality or killing another person.

Many religious people are still sinful due to the fact that they submit only *externally* to certain moral rules. Because they don't realize that they need to yield their lives to God Himself, they don't understand or reflect His true nature. They remain in rebellion against Him because they have never made a decision to turn away from their self-centered pursuits to embrace His ways. As we have seen, even a religious person may focus on doing acts that he thinks will please God, while missing the vital necessity of receiving Jesus and His sacrifice.

There isn't anyone on earth who has never harbored a selfish motive in his heart, or had a bad thought toward another person, or told a lie of some kind. These are proof enough that sin dwells in

---

[73] James 1:15.
[74] Romans 3:23.

all of us. It is impossible for anyone to refrain from committing sin (outside of receiving Jesus and relying on God's Spirit).

Sin isn't limited to extreme acts, such as engaging in blatant immorality or killing another person.

Some people, when they blame God for the bad things that happen in the world, assume the position of victim, failing to assume any responsibility for their own sinful state. Tragically, there are multitudes of innocent victims of many kinds of abuse, exploitation, and cruelty in our world. Such people need our compassion, and we must seek justice on their behalf. Sin incites, as the familiar phrase goes, "man's inhumanity to man." Yet I am speaking of those who treat God as if He is the guilty one and they are without any fault. They do not see themselves in need of His help and salvation. They do not see the problem of sin, particularly in their own lives.

In addition, much of modern psychology and psychiatry, as well as the policies and laws of some nations, does not recognize the reality of sin. Instead, it refers to various types of sinful attitudes and behavior by other terms, such as "alternative lifestyle" or "right to choose." Or, it gives other reasons for people's sinful conduct, such as "sickness," or "product of environment"; such factors may contribute to the problem, but they are not its root cause.

Consequences of Sin

We cannot end the destructive pattern of evil and death in our world if we don't deal with the root of the issue. When we understand what sin is, how it damages our lives, and why it inflicts harm on the world, we will value the sacrifice Jesus Christ made on the cross and the immense power He released on our behalf through His resurrection.

Sin offends God, and its greatest consequence is that it causes a separation between Him and us. Let's investigate several realities of sin.

1. Sin Does Not Ultimately Satisfy

Many people sin in their pursuit of some enjoyment or satisfaction in life, in an effort to fill the spiritual void in their hearts. However, some of them never experience any enjoyment in their sin; instead, they just feel empty—while they are sinning and also afterward. And, although a number of people enjoy sin at the time they engage in it, they soon discover that the pleasure is short-lived. After the initial enjoyment passes, guilt and shame often set in. Sin can never satisfy the void that comes from lacking a relationship with God, or the need for salvation that human beings carry within them.

Many people sin because they are trying to fill the spiritual void in their hearts.

---

2. Sin Hurts the One Who Commits It

When people sin, they hurt themselves the most—not only do they have to deal with the consequences of their transgressions, but they also continue to align themselves with spiritual death. "The wicked are like the troubled sea, when it cannot rest, whose waters cast up mire and dirt. 'There is no peace,' says my God, 'for the wicked.'"[75] There is no real peace for the man or woman who lives apart from God and His will, unable to escape the curse and slavery of sin.

---

[75] Isaiah 57:20–21.

3. Sin Hurts Other People

People's sin affects those around them, including—and often especially—their loved ones. Usually, people sin for selfish reasons. When they think about engaging in a sinful action, they often do not consider—or care about—the effects of their action on others. For example, when a married man commits adultery with a woman, he may think only of the immediate pleasure of the liaison, not how it will impact his spouse and children and/or those of the woman involved. The aftermath of adultery and divorce can be long-term spiritual, mental, and emotional damage, as well as financial hardships and other problems in life for those who are impacted by it.

4. Sin Often Leads to More—and Worse—Sin

Because sin usually brings only temporal satisfaction, some people seek to duplicate the short-lived feeling over and over again through additional acts of sin, creating a vicious cycle that can be very difficult to break. Moreover, committing sinful acts can awaken a greater appetite for sin, causing a person to degenerate until his behavior ultimately destroys him.

5. Sin Enslaves

When we commit sin, it becomes our master. It doesn't serve us—we serve it. "Do you not know that to whom you present yourselves slaves to obey, you are that one's slaves whom you obey, whether of sin leading to death, or of obedience leading to righteousness?"[76] Furthermore, in addition to our own sins, we carry "generational sins" in our bloodline that we inherited as a consequence of the sins of our parents, grandparents, and other ancestors.

---

[76] Romans 6:16.

We did not choose this inheritance, but it weighs heavily upon us and causes unexplained problems and failures in our lives. For example, if you look at the family line of an alcoholic, you will often discover that a parent, a grandparent, an uncle, and/or other relatives were also alcoholics.

I believe that when the Bible mentions "iniquity," it is often referring to generational sin.[77] There is absolutely nothing that you, personally, can do to get rid of iniquity. No other human being, no religion, no medical advancement or scientific discovery can deliver you from it. Only Jesus can. And, unless it is dealt with, you may pass it along to future generations.

6. Sin Leads to Death

Many people who commit sin don't believe it carries any consequences. But the Scriptures clearly state that "the wages of sin is death, but the gift of God is eternal life in Christ Jesus our Lord."[78] Because sin affects all areas of our lives, this "death" may not only be spiritual and physical alone; sometimes it can be mental or emotional or relational, and so forth.

7. Sin Incurs Punishment and Eternal Consequences

God must punish sin in order to be faithful to His nature and to the original character of the world He created. God is total goodness; He is holy (pure). If we want to know God's view of sin, we must simply look to the cross and see the punishment that He unleashed upon His own Son when Jesus took our sins upon Himself and paid the price for them on our behalf.

Either we receive Jesus as the sufficient Substitute for our sin, or we face punishment for our sins. We often suffer various negative effects in this life due to our sins. However, the

---

[77] See, for example, Deuteronomy 5:8–9.
[78] Romans 6:23.

ultimate punishment for sin will occur in the next life in the form of judgment and eternal separation from God. "And I saw the dead, small and great, standing before God, and books were opened....And the dead were judged according to their works, by the things which were written in the books."[79]

Everything we do in this life is recorded in heaven, and when we die, we will be judged in relation to our actions. There is no way to escape God's judgment for sin except by the provision of Jesus Christ. His sacrifice covers our sins, and God says He will not remember them any longer.[80] Yet sins that have not been forgiven will be exposed[81] and judged.

The good news is that when we receive Jesus and His sacrificial provision through the cross, His nature and goodness are credited to us! We know the joy and peace of being totally forgiven and cleansed from everything we have done wrong. This is what it means for us to be "righteous." Having true righteousness does not mean adopting a holier-than-thou, haughty attitude. It means receiving the nature of Jesus Himself—and this becomes our standing before God. We no longer have to fear punishment for our sin. Jesus has paid the price of that penalty for us.

While we are still alive, we have the ability to receive salvation in Jesus. However, after physical death occurs, there is no more opportunity to do so. "It is appointed for men to die once, but after this the judgment."[82] Your opportunity is here and now.

God hates sin but loves the sinner—so much so, that He came to earth in the person of Jesus to die for our sins.

---

[79] Revelation 20:12.
[80] See Hebrews 8:12.
[81] See, for example, Luke 8:17.
[82] Hebrews 9:27.

The Solution for Sin

Sin separates us from God and distorts His image in us, because all sin is the opposite of His character. The sinful nature, as well as individual sinful acts, traps in spiritual death those who have not yet received Jesus. Furthermore, when those who are born again commit sin, they will still "grieve"[83] the Holy Spirit or "quench"[84] the life of the Holy Spirit within them and therefore need to be cleansed from their sin.[85]

Jesus gave up His life to liberate us from slavery to sin. Therefore, how do we receive what He has done for us? Recall that Jesus said, "The time is fulfilled, and the kingdom of God is at hand. Repent, and believe in the gospel."[86] The solution to sin is repentance. Repentance enables us to enter God's kingdom, which is characterized not by pain and suffering but by "righteousness and peace and joy in the Holy Spirit."[87]

What Is Repentance?

Undoubtedly, many people are dissatisfied or uncomfortable with their lives and want to change them, but they don't know how to repent. One reason is that there is widespread misunderstanding about what repentance really means. Many people associate it with an emotional response like crying or feeling guilty. Others think it means doing various acts of penance to atone for one's sins, such as giving to charitable organizations or denying oneself certain pleasures. However, true repentance is not an emotional response (although emotions may accompany it). And it cannot be achieved by doing acts of penance.

---

[83] Ephesians 4:30.
[84] 1 Thessalonians 5:19.
[85] See, for example, 1 John 1:9; 2:1.
[86] Mark 1:15.
[87] Romans 14:17.

The Greek word translated as "repentance" in the New Testament indicates conviction about one's guilt, and it means "a reversal of decision." A related word signifies "to think differently." So, after an individual realizes his sinful spiritual condition, he repents by making a decision to change his wrong mind-set and attitudes about God and himself; he also commits to making a change in his behavior. He acknowledges that because of his sinful nature and sinful acts, his life is on the path to destruction, and he no longer wants to stay on that path.

Repentance has often been described as making a 180-degree turn and going in the opposite direction—*away* from sinful attitudes, immoral actions, and self-centeredness, *toward* God's character, ways, and purposes. It implies the decision to allow one's life to be governed by God without reservation—to be willing to follow and obey Him from now on.

Unless we repent, we cannot experience Christ's provision for us through the cross or receive God's Spirit. And this is crucial: only through the grace and power we receive from God's Spirit can we manifest God's nature, live according to His ways, and inherit eternal life in heaven.

When a person genuinely repents, his conduct and lifestyle are increasingly aligned with God's kingdom and priorities. Such changes are the evidence of the work of the Holy Spirit in the individual's life to draw him to God and enable him to live a righteous life. "Live by the Spirit, and you will not gratify the desires of the sinful nature."[88] We learn what pleases God by reading His Word and asking Him to teach and lead us through His Holy Spirit.

---

[88] Galatians 5:16 (NIV).

Repentance means making a 180-degree turn—away from sinful attitudes and actions, toward God's purposes and ways.

God's Kindness Leads Us to Repentance

The Scriptures say that "God's kindness leads you toward repentance."[89] Perhaps there have been times when someone has spoken to you about Jesus' love and sacrifice for you. Or maybe there have been moments when, after you have done something wrong, your conscience has bothered you, and you regretted what you did. Those were instances when God the Father's kindness was leading you to repent so that you could reach out to Him, be reconciled through Jesus, and enjoy a personal relationship with Him. He desires to be close to you. His love for you is so great that He never stops calling you and offering you salvation and a brand-new life.

Bismarck is a warehouse supervisor who experienced the kindness of God leading to repentance, forgiveness, and a new life.

"I moved to the United States from Nicaragua when I was fourteen years old. Immediately, I joined the gangs and began to consume marijuana, cocaine, and crack. I wasn't afraid of anything—I was violent and sought to experience strong emotions. Due to my lifestyle, I became homeless, and I stole to get money to buy more drugs. My addiction was such that that I even sold my own clothes and shoes for five or ten dollars, just to buy drugs.

"I was hospitalized several times for drug overdoses. I also tried to commit suicide five times. The first four times, I plunged a knife into my body. The fifth time, I hung myself with a belt. I was found lifeless, but, by a miracle of God, I revived. I believe it was because God had a purpose for my life.

---

[89] Romans 2:4 (NIV).

"At this time, I wasn't looking for Jesus, but God used someone to invite me to a house where people met to pray and learn about the Bible. Yet all I did was criticize their church and their pastor, calling him a 'thief.' I continued to criticize them until, one morning, when I was in my room, I started to feel bad about all the criticizing. I cried uncontrollably. I will never forget what happened next: I heard a Voice that said, 'That is how I wanted to see you.' The conviction from God was so strong that I could not stop crying.

"From that point, my life made an incredible turnaround. Jesus erased my past and gave me a new beginning. I had been a drug addict for twenty years, and I had been a gang member, a fornicator, and an adulterer. I feared nothing, and I didn't care about my life or anyone else's. But today, I am a man who fears God, and I feel totally restored and happy. I am employed, I take care of my home, and I serve in the church."

Steps to True Repentance

True repentance is not merely intellectual belief in God and recognition of one's sinful spiritual condition. It also involves the following steps:

1. Acknowledge and Confess Sin, with Genuine Conviction

We must honestly acknowledge before God the wrongs we have committed in thought, word, and deed, with genuine conviction for having lived in a way that is contrary to His nature. There is a book of the Bible called "Psalms," and in one of the psalms, we read: "The sacrifices of God are a broken spirit; a broken and contrite heart, O God, you will not despise."[90]

When we face God our Creator and admit to Him our sinfulness, as well as express our desire that He transform us, He activates

[90] Psalm 51:17 (NIV).

our forgiveness through Christ. The blood of Jesus, shed on the cross, becomes effective as the payment for our transgressions. The Scriptures say, "If we confess our sins, [God] is faithful and just to forgive us our sins and to cleanse us from all unrighteousness,"[91] and that "he who conceals his sins does not prosper, but whoever confesses and renounces them finds mercy."[92] God waits for us to realize the sinful condition we are in and to turn to Him for forgiveness, cleansing, and renewal.

"The sacrifices of God are a broken spirit; a broken and contrite heart, O God, you will not despise."

---

2. Make the Decision to Abandon Sin

When we genuinely repent, we turn away from activities, people, objects, and environments that influence us to sin. If we willingly place ourselves in situations that tempt us and cause us to sin, then our repentance was not genuine. We need to commit to separate ourselves from what God calls evil and wrong. And we must allow the blood of Jesus, which He shed on the cross, to break the chains of sin and iniquity that obstruct our spiritual life—as clogged arteries obstruct the flow of a person's physical blood—so that we may truly be free from sin.

Making a decision to turn away from sin does not mean we will never experience temptation or sinful thoughts again, or that we will never commit a sin again in our life. Rather, it means that we no longer desire to sin, and that sinning is no longer a habit for us. In the Bible, when Jesus forgave and healed people, He sometimes said, "Stop sinning,"[93] or "Leave your life of sin."[94] We have to leave

---

[91] 1 John 1:9.
[92] Proverbs 28:13 (NIV).
[93] John 5:14 (NIV).
[94] John 8:11 (NIV).

our lifestyle of sin, and desire to live for God, doing what pleases Him.

3. Receive God's Forgiveness Through Faith in Christ

If we repent and accept Jesus Christ as our Lord and Savior, the curse of sin is broken in our lives, and the judgment of spiritual death no longer weighs on us. We are free! Guilt and blame can no longer threaten us, and the following truth applies to us:

> There is therefore now no condemnation to those who are in Christ Jesus, who do not walk according to the flesh, but according to the Spirit. For the law of the Spirit of life in Christ Jesus has made me free from the law of sin and death.[95]

When you have repented, confessed your sin, and accepted the sacrifice of Jesus to liberate you from your sinful nature, don't continue to be enslaved by memories of your past wrongs and failings. Your bondage has ended! The freedom of Jesus Christ enables you to build a life of blessings and a heritage of freedom for your descendants and others who will inherit the consequences of your decisions.

God wants us to feel convicted by our sins so that we will go to Him and repent. He does not want us to experience continual guilt, shame, and condemnation, which will only make us want to run away from Him. Again, whenever you sin, immediately confess to God and ask forgiveness through Christ, receive His forgiveness, and renew your commitment to abandon sin and to live by the Spirit.

The Scriptures assure us, "If anyone is in Christ, he is a new creation; old things have passed away; behold, all things have become

---

[95] Romans 8:1–2.

new."[96] In Jesus, you have a brand-new nature: "You have taken off your old [sinful] self with its practices and have put on the new self, which is being renewed in knowledge in the image of its Creator."[97]

4. Believe in the Gospel of Christ

Recall that Jesus said, "Repent, and believe in the gospel."[98] It is necessary not only to experience conviction and remorse, to confess and repent of your sins, but also to actively *believe in* the gospel. The gospel is the good news of the arrival of God's kingdom on earth, which brings us freedom from sin and death. Believing completes our transformation, restoring us to God.

Believe in the gospel! You don't have to be controlled by sin, enslaved to wrong attitudes and actions. Allow God to forgive you and change your life, just as He did for Fátima García, a homemaker from the Dominican Republic:

"My encounter with Jesus came at a crucial time for me. I felt empty, emotionally alone, and without spiritual support. I had many problems in my marriage and had to divorce my husband. Additionally, I was sad over the recent death of my father, and everything looked gray to me. I fell into a deep depression and was hospitalized. I asked God to take me to be with my father. I didn't want to live anymore. My depression was so bad that I fell into a coma that lasted for six hours. When I awakened, I thought about my children and my mother, and I knew I had to live for their sake.

"My depression had caused other physical complications—high blood pressure and problems with my thyroid gland. The doctors said that I would need to be on medication for the rest of my life. When a friend learned about the condition I was in, she invited me

---

[96] 2 Corinthians 5:17.
[97] Colossians 3:9–10 (NIV).
[98] Mark 1:15.

to King Jesus Ministry. I didn't want to go, but she insisted, so I decided to go and seek God.

"When I heard the pastor's message, I felt immense peace—I had finally found Jesus! I felt deep repentance for having lived separated from Him, and I decided to turn my disastrous life over to Him so He could transform it. I continued to attend church, and, little by little, I began to realize that my life was taking a whole new direction. The prayers began to bring about a great transformation. The Lord has continued to bless me, and I have learned to pray for my children and family. In time, the doctors said I no longer needed medication, so I stopped taking it. Jesus has taught me to deal with my relationship with my children, and I have a better relationship with my ex-husband."

You don't have to be controlled by sin, enslaved to wrong attitudes and actions.

Many people run from the truth of Jesus Christ because they do not want to be confronted with their sins. But Jesus Christ cannot be received halfway. God, in His kindness, has been paving the way for you to return to Him. If you will acknowledge your sins, accept forgiveness in Jesus, turn away from a sinful lifestyle, and believe in the gospel of the kingdom, you will receive Jesus and the eternal life only He can give. You will have a brand-new nature— one that is like God's own nature. You will be reconciled to your Creator, just as if you had never sinned.

This process does not need to be complicated. It requires only a simple prayer:

Heavenly Father, I recognize that I am a sinner and that my sin separates me from You. I believe that Jesus died on the cross for me and that He was raised from the dead. I confess with my mouth that Jesus is Lord. I repent of all my sins, and I dissolve every connection that I have made—knowingly or unknowingly—with sin and with the devil. Jesus, I ask You to come into my heart and transform my life. I reject all thoughts and behaviors that do not reflect God's nature, and I ask You to enable me to walk in God's ways according to Your grace and power through the Holy Spirit. Amen!

Why believe in Jesus? Because He saved you from the grip of the sinful nature and enabled you to be forgiven for all the sins you have ever committed, providing you with a new life and an eternal relationship with God the Father!

Help Alleviate the World's Pain and Suffering

Now that you have been reconciled to God, ask Jesus daily to use you to spread God's kingdom of healing, deliverance, and righteousness in our world, alleviating people's pain and suffering.[99] We have a trustworthy promise from God that, when the fullness of His kingdom comes, "God will wipe away every tear from their eyes; there shall be no more death, nor sorrow, nor crying. There shall be no more pain, for the former things have passed away."[100]

---

[99] See Luke 4:18.
[100] Revelation 21:4.

5

A Reality We Cannot Ignore

For as long as I could remember, I had been afraid of death. This fear followed me wherever I went; the idea of losing my life terrified me. Then, I traveled to preach at a conference in Honduras, Central America, with a team of fifty people. At the end of the conference, we went to have dinner at the home of a family from the church that had invited us to come. Unknown to us, seven armed men had followed us there. While we were eating, they violently entered the house and threatened everyone at gunpoint.

Some of the men took the pastor of the church away in a car to be killed. When they arrived at the place where they were going to kill him, the pastor managed to escape. But, as he ran, he slipped and fell. At the last moment, the man who was about to shoot him received an order from one of the other men to let him go.

Meanwhile, the other armed men tied up those of us who remained at the house. They held us at gunpoint for forty-five minutes, and I prayed nonstop for God's supernatural protection. Finally, the men left. God had saved our lives.

During the time I was tied up, many questions went through my mind, such as "If I die, will I go to heaven?" "Have I done the will of God?" and "Do I have a successor for the church?" I answered all of the questions in the affirmative, and this helped me to understand that I should not fear death. In addition, I had repeated a statement from the Bible to myself that refers to followers of Jesus who were persecuted for their faith in Him: "They did not love their lives to the death."[101] As I wrote earlier, those who receive Jesus must be willing to give up their lives for Him, if necessary. It was clear to me that I hadn't been ready to do that before this incident took place. I came to understand that God had allowed me to face this situation so I could confront my fear of death and overcome it.

Today, I can go anywhere in the world, and I am not afraid to die. I know that Jesus conquered death by His sacrifice on the cross and His resurrection. And, I know that even when my body dies, my spirit will continue to live with God, and that assurance gives me absolute peace.

The Enemy of the Human Race

The ultimate prognosis of our lives is physical death. Death was not in God's original design for human beings. Yet, when the first human beings sinned, they allowed death to reign in the world.[102] Death is the enemy of the entire human race.

In today's society, more people fear death than you might imagine, to the point that they prefer not even to talk about it. Yet many people—of all cultures, nationalities, races, and social strata—are interested in and even preoccupied with the idea of death. They want to know what will happen to them after they die.

When the first human beings sinned, they allowed death to reign in the world.

---

101 Revelation 12:11.
102 See Romans 5:12–14.

Throughout history, people have expressed their fear of death in different ways, such as adopting a pessimistic attitude toward life, pursuing escapism, and developing the idea of reincarnation. According to the concept of reincarnation, after a person dies, his soul is transferred into another body (perhaps that of a newborn baby or even an animal, an insect, or an object).

When people are pessimistic, a spirit of death operates in them, so that they become apathetic or depressed and may manifest other negative attitudes. When people pursue escapism, they seek to evade reality, having their minds diverted by entertainment or other forms of pleasure; however, when they have to return to the "real world," they are often left feeling empty and frustrated. When people take hold of the idea of reincarnation, it is often an expression of their desire to correct the wrongs and failures in their life, and to believe that death is not the end for them—that they will live on in some form.

Our Two "Appointments"

Is there life after death? Definitely, yes! The Bible confirms that there is. What happens after death? We do not return to earth in a different body. There are only two possible destinations for human beings after they die. One is an eternity with God, and the other is an eternity separated from Him.

In the previous chapter, we saw that we will be judged for how we have lived during our time on earth: "It is appointed for men to die once, but after this the judgment."[103] These "appointments" are unavoidable. Do you believe it? You can miss most appointments, but there are two that you will never miss: your appointment with death and your appointment with God's judgment. God will either judge that you are righteous because you have received Jesus and your sins have been forgiven through His death on the cross, or

---

[103] Hebrews 9:27.

He will judge that you are condemned for your sin and for rejecting Him and His ways.

Do you know what awaits you after death? Do you have peace about what will happen to you after you die, or do you constantly fear an uncertain end? Jesus is the only One who not only experienced death but also won a complete victory over it. If anything differentiates true Christianity from other religions and philosophies, it is that Jesus has a *proven* answer for us concerning death.

What Happens After Death?

As we explore this topic of life after death, it is important to keep in mind that, in addition to our physical world, there is an invisible spiritual realm, which cannot be known by the natural senses. It can discerned only spiritually, and it operates according to its own laws and principles. Regardless of whether a person recognizes or believes in the spiritual realm, it still exists.

Some people think that the spiritual world exists only in the abstract, or that it is something vague and elusive. However, the reality of the spiritual world is even greater than that of the physical world. The physical realm is temporal and transitory, while the spiritual realm is eternal and permanent.[104]

Jesus told His disciples a parable in order to help them understand what occurs after death, as well as to teach them that the manner in which we conduct our lives on earth is of critical importance. In the following excerpts from that parable, we learn some of the conditions of the spiritual world that people experience when they leave the natural world through physical death. The parable begins in this way:

> There was a rich man who was dressed in purple and fine
> linen and lived in luxury every day. At his gate was laid

---

[104] See 2 Corinthians 4:18.

a beggar named Lazarus, covered with sores and longing
to eat what fell from the rich man's table. Even the dogs
came and licked his sores. The time came when the beggar died and the angels carried him to Abraham's side.
The rich man also died and was buried.[105]

The patriarch Abraham is commended by God in the Scriptures as
being a man of great faith. When the beggar Lazarus died, he was
taken to be with Abraham in a place of rest reserved for those who
manifested true faith in God and who had lived during the time
prior to Jesus' death and resurrection. After Jesus' resurrection,
heaven itself was opened to those who had died in faith, because
Jesus had accomplished their full reconciliation with God. Heaven
is where these believers now reside, along with all who have died in
faith in the centuries since Jesus' resurrection.

In contrast to Lazarus, the rich man found himself in hell, which
is the place of punishment. Let us now compare some of the char-
acteristics of the rich man and Lazarus in the afterlife.

The Personal Identity of Each One Remained the Same

"In hell, where [the rich man] was in torment, he looked up and
saw Abraham far away, with Lazarus by his side."[106] Some people
think that, after death, we lose our entire consciousness, including our identity and our memory. Others think that our existence
will merely disappear, like mist. And, as we have seen, still others
believe we will reincarnate into another body. However, according to Jesus, Lazarus and the rich man continued to be the same
people they had been on earth. Whether in heaven or in hell, in
the afterlife, people retain their consciousness, and they continue to have the same personality.

---

[105] Luke 16:19–22 (NIV).
[106] Luke 16:23 (NIV).

The physical world is temporal and transitory, while the spiritual realm is eternal and permanent.

They Recognized Each Other

"So [the rich man] called to him, 'Father Abraham, have pity on me and send Lazarus to dip the tip of his finger in water and cool my tongue, because I am in agony in this fire.'"[107] The rich man recognized Abraham, who had died thousands of years earlier. And he recognized Lazarus, who had died in his own generation. So, our consciousness, or identity, will not only remain but also be augmented, because we will no longer be limited by time and natural human senses.

They Both Remembered Their Life on Earth

"But Abraham replied, 'Son, remember that in your lifetime you received your good things, while Lazarus received bad things....'"[108] Both men apparently could remember the circumstances of what life had been like for them before they experienced physical death. After death, we, too, will be able to recall our life on earth; this means that our memory will remain in our soul. We will remember all of our past—the decisions we made, the actions we took, and the people who lived with us and around us, as well as the conditions they were in. The rich man was in hell because, during his lifetime on earth, he did not choose to follow God and His ways, and he had no compassion for his fellow man. He was reaping what he had sown.[109]

---

[107] Luke 16:24 (NIV).
[108] Luke 16:25 (NIV).
[109] See Galatians 6:7.

They Were Aware of Their Present Condition

"...but now [Lazarus] is comforted here and [the rich man is] in agony."[110] In heaven, people are aware of and enjoy their new reality. They are in the place that has been prepared for them to dwell in the fullness of life with God the Father and Jesus, apart from any pain, loneliness, sadness, or hopelessness.

In hell, people are aware of their new reality, too, which includes insatiable thirst, curses, torture, and eternal condemnation, where "their worm does not die, and the fire is not quenched,"[111] and where "there will be weeping and gnashing of teeth."[112] When a person dies without Christ, he goes directly to that place of torment. (I believe that those who have never heard the message of Jesus will be judged by God according to the knowledge they had of Him and how they responded to it. Either way, our salvation is found in Jesus alone.)

For a person who has rejected the gospel, what he will remember the most will probably be the opportunities God gave him to receive Jesus, and how he turned down those opportunities. He will have an unbearable awareness that there is nothing that can be done to alleviate his situation. His greatest torment will be his eternal separation from God and his knowledge that he can never leave that place.

There Was Complete Separation Between the Righteous and the Unrighteous

"Between us and you a great chasm has been fixed in place, so that those who want to go from here to you cannot, nor can anyone cross over from there to us."[113] Again, Lazarus and the rich man

---

110 Luke 16:25 (NIV).
111 Mark 9:44, 46, 48.
112 Matthew 8:12.
113 Luke 16:26 (NIV).

were in completely different places, and neither could cross over to where the other one was.

Heaven and Hell Are Real

My friend, heaven is a reality, but so is hell. Jesus taught more about hell than about heaven because He wanted to keep us from going to the place of eternal punishment. Hell was not created for human beings—it was made for Satan.[114] However, people who choose to live separately from God, to pursue selfish aims, and to indulge in a lifestyle of sin will receive the same punishment. That punishment reflects the true horror of sin and rebellion against God.

Because of sin, humanity's destiny—apart from salvation in Jesus Christ—is eternal death, separation from God. Therefore, if you die without Christ, your fate is hell.

Jesus taught more about hell than about heaven because He wanted to keep people from going to the place of eternal punishment.

Richard Eby was an accomplished physician and surgeon. He received Jesus as his Savior, and he was a man of faith all of his life. When he was sixty years old, he suffered a tragic accident and died, but he later came back to life and told what he had seen in the spiritual realm.

As soon as Richard died, he stopped feeling pain, and he instantly arrived in heaven, a place that was full of love, peace, and perfection. Then, Jesus told Richard that He would show him hell for two minutes by removing his name from the Book of Life.[115] Suddenly, Richard started to fall, until he landed in a pit in the center

---

[114] See Matthew 25:41.
[115] See, for example, Revelation 20:12–15.

of the earth that measured about three meters high by one meter wide and one meter deep. There was no entrance or exit, and it was absolutely silent and dark. Jesus told him that the absence of God produced the total lack of light and sound. Jesus allowed Richard to feel what would be normal sensations for a spiritual body; it was as if he had a million senses—an unlimited number. There he was, in a pit, awaiting his final judgment from God. He was terrified to know that the person who dies without Christ will instantly go to that place.

Richard could smell the stench of the demons. Suddenly, he began to hit the walls, desperate to leave because he found himself surrounded by thousands of little bodies that looked like deformed cats and dogs. They were chained and had fire for eyes. They tried to attack and terrify him; and they ridiculed him in horrible language for having rejected the Savior and for being there with them. They also said, "We will never let you leave. We will give you the hell that we are living."

Suddenly, they began to climb about his face and up the walls; they made a raucous and threatening concert, with obscene language. At one point, Richard asked them why they were there, and they answered, "We had already accepted Satan as savior, and we had no other option. We are here forever and will never leave this place."[116]

After that experience, Richard returned to life, and his story puts the fear of God into many people's hearts as they feel, much more directly, the reality of heaven and hell that waits for souls.

In another case, Mary K. Baxter had visions of hell during a thirty-day period. God gave her this gift and committed her to share her experience with the world. Accompanied by Jesus, she saw people

[116] Sid Roth and Lonnie Lane, *Heaven Is Beyond Your Wildest Expectations* (Shippensburg, PA: Destiny Image, 2012), chapter 10.

in hell who for years were called by Him to receive salvation and to carry out a special purpose, but they decided they didn't have time for it. Some preferred to have fun, while others were too busy trying to gain wealth, fame, and fortune. Now their souls are in torment. Here is a portion of what she saw:

"We came to the next pit. Inside this pit…was another skeleton form. A man's voice cried from the pit, saying, 'Lord, have mercy on me!' Only when they spoke could I tell whether the soul was a man or woman.

"Great wailing sobs came from this man. 'I'm so sorry, Jesus. Forgive me. Take me out of here. I have been in this place of torment for years. I beg You, let me out!' Great sobs shook his skeletal frame as he begged, 'Please, Jesus, let me out!' I looked at Jesus and saw that He too was crying.

"'Lord Jesus,' the man cried out from the burning pit, 'haven't I suffered enough for my sins? It has been forty years since my death.'

"Jesus said, 'It is written, *"The just shall live by faith!"* All mockers and unbelievers shall have their part in the lake of fire. You would not believe the truth. Many times My people were sent to you to show you the way, but you would not listen to them. You laughed at them and refused the gospel. Even though I died on a cross for you, you mocked Me and would not repent of your sins. My Father gave you many opportunities to be saved. If only you had listened!' Jesus wept.

"'I know, Lord, I know!' the man cried. 'But I repent now.'

"'It is too late,' said Jesus. 'Judgment is set.'

"The man continued, 'Lord, some of my people are coming here, for they also will not repent. Please, Lord, let me go tell them that they must repent of their sins while they are still on earth. I do not want them to come here.'

"Jesus said, 'They have preachers, teachers, elders—all ministering the gospel. They will tell them. They also have the advantages of the modern communications systems and many other ways to learn of Me. I sent workers to them that they might believe and be saved. If they will not believe when they hear the gospel, neither will they be persuaded though one rises from the dead.'...

"Jesus said, 'Hell is real; the judgment is real. I love them so, My child. This is only the beginning of the frightful things I have to show you. There is much more to come.

"'Tell the world for Me that hell is real, that men and women must repent of their sins....'"[117]

We Must Choose

Every member of the human race must decide whom he will follow and serve in this life—and this decision will determine the state of his existence in the next life. We will be ruled either by Jesus, who is the Truth and Giver of life, or we will be ruled by Satan, the devil, who is a liar, a thief, and a murderer. We must be cautious when making this decision, because the devil presents sin as something desirable and good. He disguises himself as an "angel of light"[118] as he seeks to trap and destroy us.

Jesus said, "The thief [devil] does not come except to steal, and to kill, and to destroy. I have come that they may have life, and that they may have it more abundantly,"[119] and "The devil...was a murderer from the beginning, and does not stand in the truth, because there is no truth in him. When he speaks a lie, he speaks from his own resources, for he is a liar and the father of it."[120] There is nothing good or generous in Satan; everything in him is perverse and

---

[117] Mary K. Baxter, *A Divine Revelation of Hell* (New Kensington, PA: Whitaker House, 1993), 27–30.
[118] See 2 Corinthians 11:14.
[119] John 10:10.
[120] John 8:44.

corrupt. His only purpose is to destroy the works of God, including the crown of God's creation—human beings.

A Liar, a Thief, and a Murderer

The devil is a liar and a thief. From the day of our birth, he dedicates himself to robbing us of every blessing that God desires for our lives. His favorite targets of destruction are the blessings of innocence, peace, joy, health, marital and family harmony, youthfulness, time, prosperity, and the worship of the true God. He desires to enslave us, and he often does so by deceiving us and encouraging us to continue sinning.

One of Satan's tactics is to tempt us in the areas in which we are weak, so that we will fall of our own choosing into his traps. His strategies are subtle, and, since we usually don't see him coming, we often don't know how, where, or through whom he will execute his plans.

The devil is also a murderer. He seeks to take away from us life in all of its forms—spiritual, emotional, mental, physical, and so on. He endeavors to kill our dreams and projects, to ruin God's purposes for us. In addition, his goal is to remove people from this world before they can discover a new life in God and carry out the purpose for which they were created. He kills people physically by inflicting sicknesses, accidents, and the worst of life's pressures on them. I believe that his influence lies behind each person who commits suicide, infanticide, abortion, parricide (the murder of one's parents), genocide, or any other type of murder.

Willie-Mae Hood is a woman who experienced Jesus' power to defeat Satan, after the devil attempted to destroy her physically. For two years, she suffered from an illness called pulmonary fibrosis (the scarring of the pulmonary tissue). Because of this disease, she had difficulty breathing and was unable to walk for long periods of time; she required help and a lot of rest.

Her situation became dire one day when she tried to walk up some stairs but couldn't catch her breath and had to be hospitalized. That night, the doctors told her that she would need to stay connected to an oxygen tank for the rest of her life. Willie-Mae responded, "No way! Jesus did not do this. Satan, take your hands off God's property!" During a time of fasting and prayer in our church, she and her daughter declared that she would receive new lungs—and a new heart, because that organ had also been affected by the disease.

When the time of fasting and prayer ended, we held a special service in the church, where Willie-Mae and her daughter anxiously expected the fulfillment of her miracle. They went to the altar, where Willie-Mae received prayer. She felt God's presence and said, "It is as if life is flowing through me." In that instant, she was filled with faith. She removed her oxygen mask and began to walk and to breathe freely. Willie-Mae shouted, "Jesus lives!" He had created new lungs and a new heart in her. All of the people exploded in celebration as they witnessed this amazing miracle. Jesus gives us abundant life, but the devil wants to rob, kill, and destroy us.

Satan's destructive campaign against human beings goes even further than physical death. He wants to devastate human beings for eternity. Jesus said, "Do not fear those who kill the body but cannot kill the soul. But rather fear Him who is able to destroy both soul and body in hell."[121]

The devil hates human beings because we have two things that he doesn't: (1) the legal right to exercise dominion on earth, which God gave to us in creation,[122] and (2) our capacity to worship God.

---

[121] Matthew 10:28.
[122] See Genesis 1:26, 28.

Satan wants to take control of the earth completely, and, above all, he desires that we worship *him*. Every time we sin, we grant the devil the right to operate in this world through us. And, every time we rebel against God and turn away from Christ—choosing an alternative purpose for living, such as the love of money, immorality, crime, or other selfish pursuits—we are, in effect, offering the devil our worship.

The devil wants to devastate human beings for eternity.

We cannot allow the devil to continue deceiving us. There is no "neutral zone." Either we are with Christ or we are with Satan. "He who sins is of the devil, for the devil has sinned from the beginning. For this purpose [Jesus] was manifested, that He might destroy the works of the devil."[123]

A Way Out

You no longer have to live as one who is condemned to hopelessness and death. There is a way out of sin, sickness, death, and hell: Jesus! "O Death, where is your sting? O [hell], where is your victory? The sting of death is sin...."[124] In this biblical quotation, what does the "sting" indicate? Figuratively, it refers to "poison." Sin is like the bite of a scorpion that injects its venom into the body of its victim, producing death.

Yet, when Jesus sacrificed His life for us on the cross, He provided an antidote to the poison of sin, and He completely defeated the devil and death. When we receive new life in Christ, we are freed from the grip of sin, and we are given power to defeat the devil's

---

[123] 1 John 3:8.
[124] 1 Corinthians 15:55–56.

attempts to entice us to sin and to destroy our lives.[125] Further-more, when we die with Christ in our hearts, we have eternal life with Him, and one day we will even be physically resurrected.[126]

Sin is like the bite of a scorpion that injects its venom into the body of its victim, producing death.

A young woman named Chrissy received freedom and a new life in Jesus after the devil tried to destroy her life emotionally, mentally, spiritually, and physically.

"My story is a hard one. My father rejected me at birth, and my mother abandoned me when I was three years old. By then, my father was in prison, so my grandmother raised me. When I was six years old, I was raped, and that incident marked my life in negative ways.

"When my father was released from prison, I moved in with him, but I found it difficult to adapt to him. I started to look for ways to escape through drugs, cigarettes, and relationships that were both physically and sexually abusive. At age sixteen, I lived on the streets, selling and using drugs. I would stay in homes of people who sold drugs and practiced lesbianism, and I was always on the verge of suffering an overdose. At age eighteen, I contracted a sexually transmitted disease. I felt like the walking dead.

"Desperate, I cried out to God and asked Him to guide me to a good church. The same week, someone told me about King Jesus Ministry. I went to a youth meeting there, and, for the first time, I felt the love and presence of God. I later attended a retreat that focused on dealing with addictions, inner healing of the soul, and generational curses. There, I felt that the power of Jesus was

---

[125] See, for example, Luke 10:19.
[126] See, for example, Romans 8:11.

setting me free from all the rejection, loneliness, abandonment, immorality, lack of love, and self-destruction in which I was living. I forgave my parents for their abandonment, and I forgave myself for all the bad things I had done to myself.

"Today, I have peace in my heart and a new life. Now, the only thing I want is for others to receive the same thing that I received from Jesus, because I know there are many people suffering, like I suffered, without finding solutions in anyone or anything. The only One who can transform a life is Jesus, the Son of God."

Why believe in Jesus? Because He died to save you from unending punishment and separation from God. Because He resurrected from the dead in order to give you a new life on earth, as well as an eternal existence in Him.

Our physical death is an inevitable fact over which we have no control. That is why we must make sure we have been reconciled to God the Father through Jesus Christ, and that we remain aligned with Him. We must not permit our hearts to grow hard, or allow a lifestyle of sin to creep back into our lives, because we don't know when or how death will arrive for us.

Today, you can make Jesus' sacrifice effective on your behalf and know that you have eternal life with God by repeating the following prayer. Pray it wholeheartedly and out loud:

> Heavenly Father, I recognize that I am a sinner and that my sin separates me from You. I believe that Jesus died on the cross for me and that He was raised from the dead. I confess with my mouth that Jesus is Lord. I repent of all my sins, and I dissolve every connection that I have made—knowingly or unknowingly—with sin and with the devil. I make the choice to follow You.

Jesus, I ask You to come into my heart and transform my life. I reject all thoughts and behaviors that do not reflect God's nature, and I ask You to enable me to walk in God's ways according to Your grace and power through the Holy Spirit. Thank You for saving me, delivering me from sin and eternal death, and giving me everlasting life with You. Amen!

6

The Great Exchange

When we receive Jesus, He becomes our very life. The Scriptures say, "I have been crucified with Christ; it is no longer I who live, but Christ lives in me; and the life which I now live in the flesh [physical body] I live by faith in the Son of God, who loved me and gave Himself for me."[127]

We begin to understand the fullness of the new life we have been given when we recognize (1) the extent to which Jesus became our Substitute, taking our sin and death on Himself, and (2) how His sacrificial death and subsequent resurrection enable us to participate right now in a great spiritual "exchange." We exchange our sinful nature for His divine nature, and all our weaknesses for His strength!

> [God has] given to us exceedingly great and precious promises, that through these [we] may be partakers of the divine nature.[128]

Let us look more closely at how this spiritual substitution and exchange came about, and what they mean for us today.

Humanity's Dilemmas

After the fall, humanity faced the following dilemmas:

---

[127] Galatians 2:20.
[128] 2 Peter 1:4.

♦ Human beings were under God's judgment, charged with sin and rebellion. "The wages of sin is death,"[129] and they had to be paid. Human beings were incapable of redeeming themselves. They could never atone for their own sins because they were all guilty: "For all have sinned and fall short of the glory of God."[130] "There is none righteous, no, not one."[131] Humanity's only option seemed to be eternal punishment and separation from God. Sinful humanity could never be reconciled to the sinless Deity; there could be no unity or agreement between them.

♦ The only way human beings could escape the sentence they deserved and receive forgiveness and cleansing was if someone else took the punishment for them and died in their place as a suitable substitute for them. However, this substitute would not only have to be another human, but he would have to be a *sinless* human. Yet the whole human race was completely infected with the sin nature.

♦ If humanity's fallen nature could not be redeemed, humans would have to remain in a perpetual, debased state of corruption and death. Their only hope would be to experience some transformation that would restore God's nature within them, allowing them to be one with Him again.

Left to their own devices, human beings were hopelessly lost and in debt to God due to their sin. The sinful nature was completely embedded in them; it was impossible for them to separate themselves from it. Furthermore, they were estranged from God and in bondage to Satan.

---

[129] Romans 6:23.
[130] Romans 3:23.
[131] Romans 3:10.

Only a sinless Substitute could take the punishment
human beings deserved because of their sin.

God's Solution

But God had a solution for humanity's dilemmas. God the Son, the second Person of the triune Deity, became a Man. He took on a physical body, experienced life as a human, showed humanity the path back to God, and then died and was raised to life again—all for our sake.

Becoming a Man enabled God to "legally" enter the earth, as well as the community of human beings, in order to restore humanity and bring back His kingdom to the world. As we have seen, God had given human beings dominion over the earth, but they forfeited it through sin, which allowed Satan to unleash destruction and death on the human race and the rest of the planet.

Why couldn't God have just created a brand-new, sinless human being who would die for us, instead of going to all the trouble of coming to earth Himself? One reason is that a newly created human being would have no vital connection with the original race of human beings who fell. That is why God the Son submitted to being born as a baby named Jesus, to an earthly mother named Mary, who was a member of the fallen race. In this way, Jesus had a direct link to the human beings who needed to be redeemed.

It is essential to understand that while Jesus was born of a human mother, He was conceived by God's Holy Spirit, so that, though a human being, He would not be infected with the sin nature. God's messenger told Mary: "The Holy Spirit will come upon you, and the power of the Highest will overshadow you; therefore, also, that Holy One who is to be born will be called the Son of God."[132]

---

[132] Luke 1:35.

Jesus' human nature was pure and without sin. This means that His human spirit was alive to God, giving Him direct communion with the Father throughout His earthly life.

A Perfect Substitute

In order to be an effective Substitute for human beings, Jesus had to experience everything we go through in life—except that He was born without sin, and He never committed sin. He had to remain sinless in the midst of a sinful world, so that He would retain His ability to be an acceptable Sacrifice for our sins. Then, when He took our sins on Himself on the cross, He experienced all the degradation of human sin. The Scriptures say, "In all things He had to be made like His brethren, that He might be a merciful and faithful High Priest in things pertaining to God, to make propitiation for the sins of the people."[133]

Of His own free will, Jesus surrendered to punishment and death on the cross for our sake. Some people think, incorrectly, that He was merely a "victim" of the religious and civil authorities of His day who insisted on His execution and carried it out. Instead, Jesus *chose* to suffer in our place, so that we would never again have to experience separation from God, and so that we would never have to endure eternal punishment. Jesus was fully aware of why He was dying, for whom He was dying, and how His death and resurrection would enact substitution and exchange. Jesus said,

> I am the good shepherd;...and I lay down my life for the sheep....No one takes it from me, but I lay it down of my own accord. I have authority to lay it down and authority to take it up again. This command I received from my Father."[134]

---

[133] Hebrews 2:17.
[134] John 10:14–15, 18 (NIV).

Jesus Set Aside His Divine Attributes to Become Human

It is amazing to realize that God the Son humbled Himself and set aside His divine attributes to rely on human resources alone, with a complete dependence on God the Father and the power of the Holy Spirit. He did this so that He could genuinely identify with human beings in all things and demonstrate how we should love and serve the Father. It is even more remarkable that Jesus would then *die* for us!

> Christ Jesus…being in the form of God, did not consider it robbery to be equal with God, but made Himself of no reputation, taking the form of a bondservant, and coming in the likeness of men. And being found in appearance as a man, He humbled Himself and became obedient to the point of death, even the death of the cross.[135]

Jesus Experienced Everything We Experience

Jesus knows what it is to be human, and therefore He understands everything you are going through right now. But He also thoroughly understands what it took to save, heal, and deliver you, and how all His provisions are available for you today. Consequently, He alone can supply the solutions to your needs and problems. Let us explore some ways in which Jesus experienced what we experience, for our sake.

Jesus understands everything you are going through right now.

---

[135] Philippians 2:5–8.

1. He Lived in a Fallen World

At the beginning of human history, the first humans had no sin, and they lived in the garden of Eden, in the presence and glory of God. However, Jesus arrived in the world when human beings and the physical Earth had been suffering the consequences of fallen humanity for thousands of years. He was born into human conditions that included pain, harshness, decadence, sickness, sorrow, and death.

2. He Lived Under Physical Conditions and Laws

Jesus came into this world like all of us do—as a baby. He had a physical body, and He grew from infancy to adulthood. He understood physical limitations, such as fatigue.[136] He was familiar with basic physical needs, such as hunger and thirst.[137] In addition, He subjected Himself to all the laws of the physical world, such as the law of gravity, the laws of motion, and so on. He also was affected by the influences of the physical environment, some of them perilous, such as dangerous storms at sea.[138]

3. He Lived Under Authority—God's and Man's Alike

Although Jesus was God, He voluntarily submitted Himself not only to the physical laws of our world but also to human and divine authority. For example, He obeyed His parents, even when they didn't understand Him.[139] He recognized human rulers for their God-given power.[140] In addition, He fulfilled all the righteousness and laws of God,[141] and He yielded fully to the Father's will.[142]

---

[136] See Mark 6:31; John 4:6.

[137] See, for example, John 4:7–8; Matthew 14:13–21.

[138] See, for example, Matthew 8:23–27.

[139] See, for example, Luke 2:41–52; John 2:1–11.

[140] See, for example, Matthew 17:24–27; Mark 12:13–17; John 19:10–11.

[141] See, for example, Matthew 3:13–16.

[142] See, for example, John 4:31–34; Matthew 26:39.

4. He Felt Human Emotions

Experiencing various emotions is a natural part of being human. One of the strongest emotions we can feel is anger. Anger itself is not a sin. The Scriptures say, "'In your anger do not sin': Do not let the sun go down while you are still angry."[143] There is such a thing as having righteous anger, for example, when we see people being treated unjustly or unmercifully. It is only when we channel our anger into destructive attitudes and behavior, such as bitterness of heart or vengeful acts, that we have crossed the line into sin.

Jesus Himself became angry at people's hypocrisy, especially when it hurt others.[144] He also became angry at injustice. For example, He drove the money changers out of the temple because they were turning it into a marketplace, just to make a profit off the people.[145]

In addition, Jesus experienced sorrow and distress. When His friend Lazarus died, Jesus grieved and wept,[146] even though He would soon raise Lazarus from the dead.[147] In the garden of Gethsemane, He was deeply troubled because He was about to surrender His soul to spiritual death and separation from God, and His body to the bloodiest of sacrifices.[148]

Every emotion that human beings feel, Jesus felt.

5. He Was Tempted

Jesus knows what it is like to be tempted to do what is wrong for purposes of self-gratification or avoiding responsibility. At the beginning of His ministry, after fasting for forty days in the wilderness, Jesus endured three intense temptations by the devil.[149]

---

[143] Ephesians 4:26 (NIV).
[144] See, for example, Matthew 23:13–15.
[145] See, for example, John 2:14–16.
[146] See John 11:32–36.
[147] See John 11:38–44.
[148] See Matthew 26:37–38.
[149] See, for example, Luke 4:1–12.

However, He never gave in to these temptations; He overcame each one by relying on the truth of God's Word[150] and the power of God's Spirit.[151] He also underwent temptation by the devil at other times.[152] Therefore, the Scriptures tell us that "we do not have a High Priest who cannot sympathize with our weaknesses, but was in all points tempted as we are, yet without sin."[153]

Jesus overcame each temptation by relying on the truth of God's Word and the power of God's Spirit.

---

6. He Knew Human Suffering and Pain

Because Jesus had a human body and lived among other human beings, He fully identified with the pain that humans suffer. The Scriptures say that He was "a Man of sorrows and acquainted with grief."[154] Jesus was often "moved with compassion" when He saw people who were sick, and He healed them.[155] When He encountered a widow burying her only son, He empathized with the deep pain of her grief, and He raised the boy from the dead.[156]

Jesus Himself experienced profound pain and suffering when He was physically tortured and crucified: He was severely whipped,[157] had His beard plucked out,[158] had a crown of thorns pressed into His head,[159] and underwent other physical abuse before suffering the excruciating death of the cross.

---

[150] See, for example, Luke 4:3–13.
[151] See, for example, Luke 4:14.
[152] See Luke 4:13.
[153] Hebrews 4:15.
[154] Isaiah 53:3.
[155] See, for example, Matthew 9:35–36; 14:14.
[156] See Luke 7:11–15.
[157] See, for example, Mark 15:15.
[158] See Isaiah 50:6.
[159] See, for example, John 19:2.

7. He Was Misunderstood, Rejected, and Betrayed

As we discussed earlier, Jesus' own family misunderstood Him.[160] In addition, He was rejected by the people of His own hometown, to the point where they even tried to kill Him.[161] He was rejected by many of the religious authorities of His day[162] and by a number of people who had once followed Him.[163] He was betrayed to the authorities by one of the disciples in His innermost circle.[164] And, when soldiers came to take Him away for trial, the rest of His closest disciples abandoned Him.[165] Then, even while He was being punished and crucified, His face was spat upon,[166] and He was ridiculed.[167]

8. He Endured Physical Death, Spiritual Death, and the "Second Death"

Jesus experienced physical death, just as every human being does. However, He especially understands the thoughts and feelings of those who die a cruel death in the prime of life, because He suffered horribly when He died.

Additionally, Jesus knew spiritual death. When He carried our sins on the cross, His human spirit was disconnected from God the Father, a separation every fallen human being has experienced. It was necessary for the Father to separate Himself from Jesus and to release His wrath on Him as the due punishment for humanity's sin and rebellion.

From my perspective, the worst pain of the cross was not the experience of the physical suffering, although that was horrible. The

---

[160] See, for example, John 7:3–5; Luke 2:41–52; John 2:1–11.
[161] See Luke 4:16–30.
[162] See, for example, Matthew 26:3–4; John 8:37–47.
[163] See John 6:60–66.
[164] See, for example, Matthew 26:14–16, 47–48.
[165] See, for example, Matthew 26:55–56.
[166] See Isaiah 50:6.
[167] See, for example, Luke 23:35–36.

most painful part for Jesus was carrying the concentration of all human sin and wickedness in His soul. The filth and rottenness of all of sinful humanity was poured onto Him. For the first time, the sinless Son of God experienced the darkness of jealousy, unforgiveness, bitterness, lies, injustice, cruelty, perversion, murder, and every other sin. He received and paid for all the actions of the human race that offend God and separate us from Him—all the sin and iniquity from the beginning of time to the very end. That is why, just before His arrest and death, He prayed, "O My Father, if it is possible, let this cup [taking on the sins of the world] pass from Me; nevertheless, not as I will, but as You will."[168]

Moreover, Jesus suffered what the Bible calls the "second death." The second death is not just physical death or even spiritual death brought about by sin. It is permanent separation from God in the next life. Jesus actually descended into hell and experienced what it means to be punished for sin in eternity, and He did that for all of us.[169] There, He received God's wrath for the sins and iniquity of the entire human race.

Jesus had to descend even to hell itself to experience the full punishment for humanity's sin—everything human beings would experience without His salvation and grace—so that He could be a faithful and true Savior for us. Jesus allowed Himself to be unjustly accused, arrested, judged, mocked, tortured, crucified, and killed. He did it all as our Substitute, because He knew that His death would pay for our sin; and because it was the *only way* to break the curse of sin and iniquity that weighed on us and separated us from God the Father.

Jesus' substitutionary sacrifice on our behalf was complete, sufficient, and final. He suffered and died once for all people. Now, He never again has to endure God's punishment and wrath. And

---

[168] Matthew 26:39.
[169] See, for example, Ephesians 4:9; 1 Peter 3:18–20.

neither does any other human being who receives Jesus and His sacrifice for him.

> But we see Jesus, who was made a little lower than the angels, now crowned with glory and honor because he suffered death, so that by the grace of God he might taste death for everyone.[170]

> Christ, having been raised from the dead, dies no more. Death no longer has dominion over Him. For the death that He died, He died to sin once for all; but the life that He lives, He lives to God.[171]

Jesus was temporarily cut off from spiritual union with God the Father so that we could receive His life.

Jesus Was Resurrected to Give Us Life

Jesus experienced all of the above for us. Then, He was raised from the dead, and we can now experience the fullness of His resurrection life! This is how He provides us with the great exchange. He gives us His spiritual and physical life in place of our spiritual and physical death.

The essence of the cross consists in Jesus taking our place. He personally suffered the totality of the punishment we deserved. In exchange, we receive forgiveness, as well as all of Jesus' righteousness and the blessings of His obedience to the Father. Today, we can live according to His life in us, receiving all the benefits of His work on our behalf, including salvation, healing, and freedom from the devil's oppression.

---

[170] Hebrews 2:9 (NIV).
[171] Romans 6:9–10.

Jesus was "delivered up because of our offenses, and was raised because of our justification."[172] To be "justified" means that although we were guilty, we have been made righteous before God in Christ, just as if we had never sinned. We are justified only by means of faith in the effectiveness of Jesus' death and resurrection for us.

Let us look at some results and blessings of the great exchange:

Results and Blessings of the Great Exchange

+ Jesus was wounded so that we could be forgiven: "He was wounded for our transgressions, He was bruised for our iniquities."[173]

+ Jesus carried our sicknesses and suffered our sorrows so that we could receive healing: "Surely He has borne our griefs (sicknesses, weaknesses, and distresses) and carried our sorrows and pains [of punishment]....With the stripes [that wounded] Him we are healed and made whole."[174]

+ Jesus *became* sin for us, receiving our punishment, so that we could be made righteous: "For [God] made [Jesus] who knew no sin to be sin for us, that we might become the righteousness of God in Him."[175]

+ Jesus died in our place and was resurrected so that we could share in His eternal life: "Reckon yourselves to be dead indeed to sin, but alive to God in Christ Jesus our Lord."[176]

---

[172] Romans 4:25.
[173] Isaiah 53:5.
[174] Isaiah 53:4–5 (AMP).
[175] 2 Corinthians 5:21
[176] Romans 6:11.

+ Jesus paid for our poverty so that we could be prosperous: "For your sakes He became poor, that you through His poverty might become rich."[177]

+ Jesus suffered our shame so that we could partake of His glory: "It was fitting for Him, for whom are all things and by whom are all things, in bringing many sons to glory, to make the captain of their salvation perfect through sufferings."[178]

+ Jesus suffered our rejection so that we could be accepted by God: "To the praise of the glory of His grace, by which He made us accepted in the Beloved."[179]

In fulfillment of the above truths, I have seen many people saved, healed, and delivered. When we understand the perfect work of the cross and the resurrection, we can begin receiving all its benefits, including God's supernatural power in our lives.

Jesus Restored What Humanity Had Lost

Jesus experienced our life so that we could experience His. As He achieved the great exchange, He restored everything that humanity had lost when the first human beings turned their backs on God and sinned. Let us look at several areas in which we have been restored.

1. Restored to Our Union and Fellowship with God the Father

The culmination of the perfect work of Christ on the cross and His glorious resurrection is our restoration to the presence of God. Jesus was cut off from God the Father on the cross so that we could live with the Father for all eternity. Through Jesus, we have

---

[177] 2 Corinthians 8:9.
[178] Hebrews 2:10.
[179] Ephesians 1:6.

union with the Father once more, giving us access to His spiritual life. "He who is joined to the Lord is one spirit with Him."[180] Our union and fellowship with God can be enjoyed in the present, not just in the future. Because of Jesus, we have continual access to God in His glory, and we have oneness with Him now and forever. This would not be possible if Jesus had not died for us and risen victoriously from the grave.

Jesus experienced our life so that we could experience His.

---

2. Restored to a Physical Body That Manifests the Life of God

This manifestation has two aspects:

1. Jesus' Resurrection Life in Our Bodies, Right Now

The Scriptures tell us: "If the Spirit of Him who raised Jesus from the dead dwells in you, He who raised Christ from the dead *will also give life to your mortal bodies through His Spirit who dwells in you*."[181] I believe this statement indicates that we can have total physical health while we live on this earth. First, as we noted in the bulleted statements above, when Jesus died, He carried all of our sins *and* all of our sicknesses. Second, since God's Spirit dwells within us and gives us abundant life, our bodies should not remain sick.

In my ministry, I have seen physical healings by Jesus' resurrection power in the lives of the people for whom we pray in His name. For example, a Venezuelan woman named Eusselin had suffered from degenerative rheumatoid arthritis for twenty-three years.

---

[180] 1 Corinthians 6:17.
[181] Romans 8:11.

During the last year of her illness, she was bedridden. As Eusselin searched for a solution, the doctors operated on her knees, but she later suffered the total wearing down of her right hip bone, and, in just a few months, she was wheelchair bound. She was unable to get out of the chair on her own, or even place her feet on the floor. Furthermore, she suffered from kidney problems and had to start using diapers because she couldn't control her bladder.

It was in this condition that Eusselin went to the home of a believer who had invited her to watch a healing service broadcast from our Miami church via satellite. During the time of worship, I began to declare the power of Christ's resurrection. Eusselin, who was watching from Venezuela, heard God's voice audibly telling her, "Rise up from the wheelchair!" Immediately, she stood up! The next thing she did was use the bathroom. She was instantly healed of both diseases, having experienced creative miracles in her right hip and her kidney. Later, her entire family came to believe in the living Jesus and in His power to do miracles.

The resurrection life of Jesus even raises the dead today. Here is the testimony of César Augusto Atoche, a Peruvian pastor:

"I was hospitalized in Lima, Peru, because my coronary artery was blocked, and I needed bypass surgery. During the operation, after my chest had been open for three hours, I suffered a heart attack and died. I was dead for a period of one hour.

"Later, the doctors told me that my heart had stopped beating and that my wife had been informed that I had died due to complications during surgery. My wife told me afterward that prior to the surgery, she had felt deep within her that I would die but that I would also be resurrected. She made a covenant with God through a Christian television program and shared the covenant with an administrator of that program who was also a friend of hers. Together with the leaders from our church, this administrator helped my wife to pray for me.

"During the hour in which I was dead, Apostle Guillermo Maldonado was on his television program praying for healing, decreeing that all the sick would rise and be healed. At that moment, I came back to life. Jesus Christ resurrected me! My wife and the doctors were amazed. One of the signs that will follow those who believe in Christ is that the dead will resurrect.[182] I am one of them!"

In another case, a twenty-month-old baby named Kevin suffered a high fever with convulsions and was hospitalized in Chicago. The doctors determined that his organs were weak, and soon the heart monitor registered that the baby had suffered a heart attack. As hard as they tried, the doctors were unable to save the boy, and they pronounced him dead.

The baby's mother, Magali, held her deceased son in her arms, and she phoned the baby's grandmother, a believer who lived in Florida. Immediately, the grandmother contacted her pastor, Freddy Lagos, of Naples, Florida, who is associated with King Jesus Ministry. The pastor began to pray through the telephone for the baby, rebuking the spirit of death and declaring life, in the name of Jesus. Suddenly, the grandmother began to scream because she was informed that the baby's monitor was registering heartbeats again. The breathing pump also began to work, indicating that the baby was breathing again. Color returned to his face, and his body temperature normalized. Kevin had come back to life after eleven minutes of being clinically dead!

I continually witness miracles of salvation, healing, and deliverance that Christ's death and resurrection bring to the lives of those who accept Him as Lord and Savior. If sickness has robbed your health; if bitterness has taken your joy; if your inability to restore your relationship with your spouse, children, or parents has discouraged you; or if it seems impossible for you to overcome the

---

[182] See, for example, Matthew 10:8.

spiritual void within you, the solution is to receive the exchange Jesus offers.

Many people in this world suffer greatly. They endure much pain, abuse, rejection, and loneliness, not knowing that Jesus gave up His life to give them freedom and peace. Jesus wants to make Himself real in your heart today, manifesting His transforming power—first in your spirit, and then in your relationships, finances, health, vocation, and all other aspects of your life.

2. Eternal Resurrection Bodies

Jesus will not only give life to our mortal bodies today. When He comes to earth a second time to judge the world and to gather those who believe in Him to be with Him always,[183] each believer will be transformed to be like Him, receiving a glorified, eternal body![184]

> We shall not all sleep [die], but we shall all be changed—in a moment, in the twinkling of an eye, at the last trumpet. For the trumpet will sound, and the dead will be raised incorruptible, and we shall be changed. For this corruptible must put on incorruption, and this mortal must put on immortality.[185]

> Beloved, now we are children of God; and it has not yet been revealed what we shall be, but we know that when He is revealed, we shall be like Him, for we shall see Him as He is.[186]

---

[183] See, for example, 2 Timothy 4:1.
[184] See, for example, 1 Thessalonians 4:14–17; 1 Corinthians 15:42–44, 49–53.
[185] 1 Corinthians 15:51–53.
[186] 1 John 3:2.

3. Restored to Rule and Reign on Earth

In addition to restoring our union with the Father and restoring the health and life of our physical bodies, Jesus came to restore to earth the kingdom of God in all its aspects. Sin, demons, poverty, death, and all other ills that we experience are the results of the fall of humanity and the influence of Satan in the world. They need to be exchanged for the life of Jesus. When Jesus was on earth, He confronted these elements with the superiority of God's kingdom, and He was always victorious.

Through His death and resurrection, Jesus won a complete victory over sin and Satan; He took from the devil the keys of hell and death.[187] Satan was absolutely, irrevocably, and eternally defeated. Jesus' complete victory applies to us because He won it for us. That is why, over a period of forty days after His resurrection, Jesus taught His disciples concerning the kingdom of God.[188] He wanted them to understand what the kingdom is and how they were called to increase its influence in the world. And, He wants us to understand the same.

Jesus came to restore the kingdom of God to earth.

After these forty days of teaching, Jesus returned to God the Father in heaven. "Looking unto Jesus, the author and finisher of our faith, who for the joy that was set before Him endured the cross, despising the shame, and has sat down at the right hand of the throne of God."[189] Today, Jesus sits at the right hand of the Father, having all power and authority over the spiritual and natural worlds alike.

---

[187] See, for example, Revelation 1:18.
[188] See Acts 1:1–3.
[189] Hebrews 12:2.

Just before returning to the Father, Jesus told His disciples, "All authority has been given to Me in heaven and on earth."[190] The Father gave Him complete authority. In turn, Jesus gives us His authority to use in His name, so that we can increase God's kingdom on earth.[191] As we receive Jesus and walk in His authority, we can live as He lived. We can defeat Satan's attempts to rob, kill, and destroy people, exchanging his evil works for kingdom works of love, power, healing, hope, and restoration.

We can do all these things because Jesus not only gave us His authority, but He also gave us His power to carry out that authority. He said, "But you shall receive power when the Holy Spirit has come upon you; and you shall be witnesses to Me in Jerusalem, and in all Judea and Samaria, and to the end of the earth."[192] Jesus also said, "Most assuredly, I say to you, he who believes in Me, the works that I do he will do also; and greater works than these he will do, because I go to My Father."[193]

We are meant to do the same good works that Jesus did on earth. We can do those works and even "greater works" because Jesus has given us the gift of the Holy Spirit. God's Spirit is always with us to guide us in the truth and to give us the power to do God's will. The only condition is that we remain united with Jesus, manifesting His nature and following His ways.[194]

Receive the Exchange by Faith

Why believe in Jesus? Because He died and was resurrected so that you could have access to the fullness of God's abundant life in all its facets. Jesus is alive! Every provision He secured by His death and resurrection is available right now for those who receive

---

[190] Matthew 28:18.
[191] See, for example, Matthew 28:19–20.
[192] Acts 1:8.
[193] John 14:12.
[194] See John 15:4–5, 7 (NIV).

Him in their hearts and confess Him as Lord and Savior of their lives. All they need to do is to claim, by faith, His great exchange— exchanging their sin for His righteousness, their death for His life, their sickness for His health, and their oppression for His freedom.

This may be the most important moment of your life. Allow the Giver of life the opportunity to grant you eternal life. If you will receive Jesus wholeheartedly, you will realize that the sole purpose of this book is to give you the most valuable gifts a human being can ever receive—a new life in Jesus on earth and an existence in the presence of God for eternity. You can receive Jesus and His great exchange by saying this prayer with sincerity and humbleness:

> Heavenly Father, I believe that Jesus died on the cross for me and that He was raised from the dead. I confess that He is my Savior and Lord. By faith, I claim Jesus' great exchange—exchanging my sin for His righteousness, my death for His life, my sickness for His health, and my oppression for His freedom. Thank You that I am "born of God," that I have entered Your kingdom, and that I now live in the fullness of Jesus' life. Please use me to spread Your kingdom in this world, carrying Your salvation, healing, deliverance, and miracles to others. Amen!

7

Who Is Jesus?

I s it more appropriate to ask, "Who is Jesus?" or "Who was Jesus?"

Jesus of Nazareth is as much a contemporary figure as He is a historical one. As a human being, He did not remain in the grave after being put to death on the cross. He was resurrected, having secured our salvation and reconciliation with the Father. As God, He is not limited by the past or the future; nor can these terms be applied to Him. Rather, He *is*!

The living Jesus is the most powerful influence in the world today— not just because of His historical impact but also because of His ability to transform lives, like yours and mine, right now and for eternity. Therefore, it is entirely appropriate for us to refer to Him in the present tense. Jesus was, Jesus is, and Jesus will always be the same to us—today, tomorrow, and forever!

The living Jesus is the most powerful influence in the world today.

In Search of a Better Future

Hundreds of millions of people throughout the centuries have encountered the living Jesus through a personal relationship with Him. The following is the testimony of business owner Ricardo Gutiérrez.

"I escaped Cuba's regime by raft, risking my life to come to America in search of a better future. However, that 'better future' was not to be. I had been a humble, innocent, and noble young man. But when I turned twenty-two, I started going to clubs, where I tried drugs for the first time. That was the beginning of my addiction and, along with it, my disorderly living. I would spend my days and nights in the club. I also became a con man, ruining many lives.

"One day, at a party, I took a mixture of three types of drugs, and I suffered cardiac arrest. I passed out, as if I were dead. Very few people survive an acid overdose, but I believe Jesus raised me up. My lifestyle affected my family greatly. My mother contracted cancer, probably from suffering so much, and my father got a tumor and was given three months to live.

"Then, a friend who formerly did drugs with me invited me to church. By that time, I was in total depression. Twice, I had tried to kill myself, but I didn't have the strength to go through with it. At church, the pastor's words seemed specific for my life. My friend took me by the arm and led me to the altar. They prayed for me, and something changed in me. Jesus had entered my life and would change it forever.

"That day, the presence of God brought tears to my eyes. Crying, I asked my mother to forgive me. Since that day, my life has straightened out. I finished high school and then joined the police department. I also have my own business. I got married and now have a beautiful family. I don't have any type of bad habit, and there is peace in my heart. My parents converted to Christianity thanks to the great transformation they saw in me. My life radically changed on the day I had an encounter with the resurrected Jesus."

The resurrected Jesus can transform your life, too, if you will give Him the opportunity. The following account from Colombian-American student Alan Correa is another testimony of a life changed by Jesus.

"I come from a family that was in complete disorder, with drug addiction, alcoholism, violence, and generational curses of poverty, anger, pride, rebellion, sexual immorality, and confusion. When I was about seventeen, influenced by the people around me, I began to steal and sell drugs. This made it easy for me to dedicate myself to a life of crime and vileness.

"The state of my life at that time may be illustrated by the following incident, which remained engraved in my memory. On a certain occasion, a young lady offered herself to me to be sold for money, and so I prostituted her. The following morning, when I thought about what I had done for just a couple of dollar bills, I felt disgusted with myself. Even though she was older than I and was used to doing this, it was not the life I would have wanted for any woman in my family. And yet, I continued doing it for money.

"I was following in my father's footsteps. I often felt that I would die having wasted my life, and I didn't want to end up like my father, killing myself with a bullet. I didn't want to take my life, but I knew that someone eventually would if I continued my lifestyle.

"One day, a friend invited me to church. He would always encourage me to go, and I would always refuse. When I finally confessed Jesus as my Lord, a great yearning to know more about Jesus and the Bible began to grow in me. I was water baptized and later attended a Christian conference at which the presence of God became palpable in my life. God showed me His power! My body began to sweat, and I experienced something that felt like a strong shock of electricity. For a moment, I was afraid and said, 'Lord, please stop!' But His power only became stronger upon me.

"That experience transformed my life forever! I had encountered the true Jesus. I was set free of the generational curses of self-destruction, crime, and drug addiction. It has been over a year since I started to serve Jesus, taking His message and demonstrating the power of God to people who need it. I know that my destiny has changed for the good! Today, I can say that I have true life!"

The resurrected Jesus can transform your life if you will give Him the opportunity.

"He Who Calls You Is Faithful"

Why believe in Jesus? Throughout this book, we have seen that Jesus is the Way, the Truth, and the Life. He has freed us from the grip of the sinful nature and enabled us to be forgiven for all the sins we have ever committed. He has rescued us from unending punishment. He has given us a new life and an eternal relationship with God the Father. And, He has given us access to God's abundant life in all its facets through the great exchange of His life for ours.

When we answer Jesus' invitation to follow Him, He requires that we give Him everything—our entire life. That is the only way for us to receive the fullness of life that He offers us. Jesus said,

> If anyone desires to come after Me, let him deny himself, and take up his cross daily, and follow Me. For whoever desires to save his life will lose it, but whoever loses his life for My sake will save it. For what profit is it to a man if he gains the whole world, and is himself destroyed or lost?[195]

Will you acknowledge Jesus as your all-sufficient Savior and absolute Lord? Yes, there are costs to following Jesus. But the rewards are true life in this world and true life for eternity. Additionally, Jesus knows that you cannot follow Him without His constant

---

[195] Luke 9:23–25.

presence and help, and He has assured you, "I will never leave you nor forsake you."[196] The Scriptures say, "Now may the God of peace Himself sanctify you completely; and may your whole spirit, soul, and body be preserved blameless at the coming of our Lord Jesus Christ. *He who calls you is faithful, who also will do it.*"[197] God will enable you to remain faithful to Jesus as you obey Him and learn to live in the power of the Holy Spirit.

Jesus said, "I will never leave you nor forsake you."

Who Is Jesus to You?

The question "Who is Jesus?" is one that people have asked for thousands of years. In fact, Jesus once inquired of His disciples, "Who do men say that I, the Son of Man, am?"[198] The disciples gave various answers regarding what the people of Jesus' day were mistakenly saying about Him.[199] Jesus then asked His disciples, "But who do you say that I am?"[200] The disciple Peter answered, "You are the Christ, the Son of the living God."[201]

Peter was able to answer this question accurately, but not because of his own insightfulness. Jesus told Peter, "Flesh and blood has not revealed this to you, but My Father who is in heaven."[202] God the Father, through the Holy Spirit, had revealed to Peter the truth that Jesus was His Son, "the Christ," a term that means "anointed."

---

[196] Hebrews 13:5.
[197] 1 Thessalonians 5:24.
[198] Matthew 16:13.
[199] See Matthew 16:14.
[200] Matthew 16:15.
[201] Matthew 16:16.
[202] Matthew 16:17.

We, too, need a revelation by God's Spirit regarding who Jesus is. Jesus said, "No one can come to Me unless the Father who sent Me draws him; and I will raise him up at the last day."[203]

In the introduction to this book, we saw that people today have various and diverse opinions about who Jesus is. Some think of Him primarily as a great philosopher, prophet, teacher, or spiritual guide. Others consider Him merely a loving and generous historical personage. But many people recognize and believe in Jesus as God, who came to earth as a Man to die for us and who returned to heaven after being raised from the dead, changing the course of human history and transforming hearts and lives even today.

Now, who do *you* say that Jesus is? You must decide.

---

[203] John 6:44.

For questions or more information, please contact:
King Jesus International Ministry
(Ministerio Internacional El Rey Jesús):
http://kingjesusministry.org/
http://www.elreyjesus.org/